——— History and Program ———

History and Program
Revised and Updated

Margaret Rowland Post
REVISED BY THOMAS E. DIPKO

UNITED CHURCH PRESS®

Cleveland

United Church Press
700 Prospect Avenue
Cleveland, Ohio 44115
unitedchurchpress.com

© 1986, 1991, 2007 United Church Press

Printed in the United States of America on acid free paper
that contains post-consumer fiber

11 10   19 18 17

ISBN: 978-0-8298-1763-8

Contents

Preface

The union of the Evangelical and Reformed and the Congregational Christian Churches in 1957 sought to give visible expression to Christ's prayer in the gospel of John, "that they may all be one." This church, now in its fifth decade, continues to be deeply committed to the unity of the universal church even as it seeks to identify its unique place in God's mission in the world. In the pages that follow, I hope that you will gain a new appreciation for the rich and varied traditions that make up the United Church of Christ and that you will discover the exciting ways this church engages the world with the Good News of Jesus Christ.

The local church has been and continues to be the basic unit of mission and ministry in the United Church of Christ. These communities of faith, gathered together under the Word to discern God's will and way for mission, work in covenant with Associations; Conferences; national Covenanted, Associated, and Affiliated Ministries; church related colleges; seminaries; health and human service institutions; and ecumenical and global partners to participate in a mission that is as old as the Gospel extending throughout the world. Calling children and adults to faith through evangelical witness; preparing for baptism and Bible study; gathering for spirited worship centered in the preaching of the Word and the celebration of Holy Communion; responding as Jesus did to human need by caring for those who hurt; and speaking and acting for justice in our society like the prophets of ancient Israel, continue to be the shared responsibility of every setting of the United Church of Christ.

Recognizing that Jesus Christ is the head of the church, the United Church of Christ has claimed as its own the faith of the church through the ages, even as it has understood the responsibility of each generation to claim and confess that faith in the face of new circumstances. Our world is very different from the world our founders sought to address. The exciting growth of racial and ethnic diversity across North America, Puerto Rico, and Hawaii; the reality of our global economy with all its promise and pain; the visible presence of persons of other faiths in almost every community; and the dramatic political and social changes in Europe, Africa, Asia, and Latin America challenge us in ways our forebears in the 1950s could have hardly imagined. Yet we remain what we have always been at our best, a people bearing witness to a grand moral vision rooted in the Bible and the person of the crucified and risen Christ, and a people of spiritual audacity, prepared to risk old assumptions for the sake of new possibilities.

I trust you will sense in the dynamic history and exciting program described in this booklet an invitation to your own deepened involvement in the faith, life, and witness of the United Church of Christ.

JOHN H. THOMAS
General Minister and President

Statement of Faith

We believe in you, O God, Eternal Spirit, God of our Savior Jesus Christ and our God, and to your deeds we testify:

You call the worlds into being,
    create persons in your own image,
    and set before each one the ways of life and death.
You seek in holy love to save all people from aimlessness and sin.
You judge people and nations by your righteous will
    declared through prophets and apostles.
In Jesus Christ, the man of Nazareth, our crucified
    and risen Savior,
    you have come to us
    and shared our common lot,
    conquering sin and death
    and reconciling the world to yourself.
You bestow upon us your Holy Spirit,
    creating and renewing the church of Jesus Christ,
    binding in covenant faithful people of all ages,
    tongues, and races.
You call us into your church
    to accept the cost and joy of discipleship,
    to be your servants in the service of others,
    to proclaim the gospel to all the world
    and resist the powers of evil,
    to share in Christ's baptism and eat at his table,
    to join him in his passion and victory.
You promise to all who trust you
    forgiveness of sins and fullness of grace,
    courage in the struggle for justice and peace,
    your presence in trial and rejoicing,
    and eternal life in your realm which has no end.
Blessing and honor, glory and power be unto you. Amen.

Approved by the Executive Council in 1981 for use in the United Church of Christ in connection with the 25th anniversary.

A History of the
United Church of Christ

All Christians are related in faith to Judaism and are faith descendants of the first apostles of Jesus who roamed the world with the good news of God's love. Within five centuries, Christianity dominated the Roman Empire. Until A.D. 1054 when the church split, it remained essentially one. Since that time, the Eastern Orthodox Church has continued its center at Constantinople (Istanbul), the Roman Catholic Church at Rome.

During the 16th century, when Christians found the church corrupt and hopelessly involved in economic and political interests, leaders arose to bring about reform from within. The unintended by-product of their efforts at reform was schism in the western church. Their differences over the authority and practices of the Roman Catholic Church became irreconcilable.

Protestant reformers such as Martin Luther, Ulrich Zwingli, and John Calvin held that the Bible, not the Pope, was sufficient authority as the word of God. Paramount was the message of Paul that persons are justified by the grace of God through faith alone. Such faith did not lead to rank individualism or moral indifference, but to good works out of love for God.

Protestantism spread throughout Europe. Lutheran churches were planted in Germany and throughout Scandinavia; the Re-formed churches, originating in Switzerland, spread into Germany, France, Transylvania, Hungary, Holland, England, and Scotland. The United Church of Christ traces its roots back to those movements to proclaim the good news based on biblical truths led by the Spirit of God. It presently binds in covenant 5,750 congregations with approximately 1,300,000 members. One of the youngest American denominations, its background also makes it one of the oldest in Protestantism.

The United Church of Christ, a *united* and *uniting* church, was born on June 25, 1957 out of a combination of four groups. Two of these were the *Congregational Churches* of the English Reformation with Puritan New England roots in America, and the *Christian Church* with American frontier beginnings. These two denominations were concerned for freedom of religious expression and local autonomy and united on June 17, 1931 to become the Congregational Christian Churches.

The other two denominations were the *Evangelical Synod of North America*, a 19th-century German-American church of the frontier Mississippi Valley, and the *Reformed Church in the United States*, initially composed of early 18th-century churches in Pennsylvania and neighboring colonies, unified in a Coetus in 1793 to become a Synod. The parent churches were of German and Swiss heritage, conscientious carriers of the Reformed and Lutheran traditions of the Reformation, and united to form the Evangelical and Reformed Church on June 26, 1934.

The Evangelical and Reformed Church and the Congregational Christian Churches shared a strong commitment under Christ to the freedom of religious expression. They combined strong European ties, early colonial roots, and the vitality of the American frontier church. Their union required accommodation between congregational and presbyterial forms of church government. Both denominations found their authority in the Bible and were more concerned with what unites Christians than with what divides them. In their marriage, a church that valued the free congregational tradition was strengthened by one that remained faithful to the liturgical tradition of Reformed church worship and to catechetical teaching. A tradition that maintained important aspects of European Protestant-ism was broadened by one that, in mutual covenant with Christ, embraced diversity and freedom.

OUR REFORMATION ROOTS

There were harbingers of the Reformation before the 15th century. In England, John Wyclif translated the Bible into English in 1382 so that all people could have access to it. John Hus encountered Wyclif's translation and writings when returning Oxford students brought them to the University of Prague from which he was graduated in 1394. After furthering the cause of biblical access and authority and opposing the Catholic sale of indulgences, Hus was burned in 1415. He claimed that Christ, not the Pope, was the head of the church; the New Testament, not the church, was the final authority; the Christian life was to be lived in poverty, not opulence.

In 1517, the German monk, university teacher, and preacher, Martin Luther nailed 95 theses of protest against certain doctrines and practices (such as the sale of indulgences) of the Roman Catholic Church to the door of the Wittenberg cathedral. His subsequent teaching, preaching, and writing spread Lutheran reform throughout northern Europe.

Almost simultaneously, Reformation winds blew to France and Switzerland. In Zurich, Ulrich Zwingli (1484–1531) and in Geneva, John Calvin (1509–64) took up the banner of reform. Their powerful ministries impressed leaders from Europe and Britain seeking a better way. From these churches of Switzerland, the German Reformed movement and the English Congregationalists would breathe deeply.

The Reformed churches differed from the Lutheran churches in avoiding the "Catholic use" of imagery and instrumental music. They differed in their interpretation of the Lord's Supper; rather than being the body and blood of Christ, Reformed faith held that the bread and wine were "seals" or remembrances of Christ's spiritual presence.

Luther and Zwingli had other differences besides their interpretations of the elements of Communion. Zwingli was more of a humanist and Luther considered his political activism dangerously radical and theologically unsound.

French refugee John Calvin arrived in Geneva, crossroads for exiles and expatriots, in 1536. He rapidly became more influential than Zwingli, second only to Luther. He wrote a popular, systematic presentation of Christian doctrine and life, *The Institutes* (1536, final edition in 1559). Most important of Calvin's *Institutes* was obedience to God's will as defined in the scriptures. Salvation, he wrote, came by faith in God's grace, mediated through word and sacrament by the power of the Holy Spirit. Good works were consequences of union with Christ in faith, not the means of salvation. Calvin considered the law an indispensable guide and spur to the Christian life; prayer provided nourishment for faith. He argued that faith was a divine gift resulting from God's unconditional decree of election.

Further, Christian life was maintained by the institutions of the church, the sacraments of Holy Communion and baptism, and discipline. Calvin followed the biblical model in providing pastoral care and church discipline through pastors, teachers, elders, and deacons.

The Reformed faith eventually reached the German Palatinate around Heidelberg. Elector Frederick III (1515–76) was forced to mediate between his own warring Zwinglian and Lutheran chaplains; he dismissed them both. Sympathetic to Calvinism, Frederick entrusted the writing of a new confession to two young protégés of Calvin and Melancthon, Casper Olevianus (1536–87) and Zacharias Ursinus (1534-83). The result was the remarkable *Heidelberg Catechism*, adopted in 1563, that unified the German Reformed Church and became a treasured resource for instructing the young, for preaching, and for theological teaching.

There also was wider social unrest in Europe. From 1618 to 1648, the Thirty Years War ravaged the continent. Before the fighting ceased, most of Germany, and especially the Palatinate where the Reformed Church had been influential, was reduced to a wilderness. Churches were closed, many pastors and people starved or were massacred. The Peace of Westphalia in 1648 divided the spoils. The Roman, Lutheran, and Reformed churches were allowed to reclaim territories that had been theirs in 1624. Calvinist Reformed churches, for a time unrecognized, were honored along with Lutheran churches.

Protestantism in Germany had lost all its eastern territory. When two thirds of Hungary was regained for Roman Catholicism, Hungarian Reformed Church Christians suffered intolerance. Their descendants emigrated to America and in 1890 began the first Hungarian Reformed Church in Cleveland. As the Magyar Synod, Hungarian churches united with the Reformed Church in the United States in 1921. Twenty-eight congregations continue in the United Church of Christ as the Calvin Synod.

The German Evangelical Movement

No one liked the Westphalian settlement, but the lines were drawn, the sixteenth century Reformation was over. Germany lay devastated, plundered by lawless armies, much of its population decimated. Commerce and industry had disappeared; moral, intellectual, and spiritual life had stagnated. Religion was dispirited and leaderless. A time for mystics and poets, much of German hymnody comes from this early 17th century.

Out of such sensitivities, a new Protestant movement, Pietism, arose. Pietism became the heart of a number of Lutheran-Reformed unions. In 1817, the Evangelical Church of the Prussian Union, by order of Frederick William III (1797–1840) of Prussia, united the Lutheran and Reformed Churches of his kingdom, giving birth to the ancestral church of the Evangelical Synod of North America, a grandparent of the United Church of Christ. The Evangelical Church of the Prussian Union became a model in other German kingdoms for Lutheran and Reformed unions. In 1981, the United Church of Christ recovered these roots when a *Kirchengemeinschaft* (church communion) with representative leaders of that church from the German Democratic Republic and the Federal Republic of Germany acknowledged with joyous celebration full communion with the United Church of Christ at the 13th *General Synod*.

The pathetic human condition in war-torn 17th century Germany awakened Pietism, a theology of the heart, balanced by moral stringencies for self-discipline. The Pietist movement was initiated by Philip Jacob Spener (1635–1705), a Lutheran pastor sensitive to the needs of his congregation demoralized by war. Drunkenness and immorality were rife, church services sterile. Spener inspired a moral and spiritual reformation, emphasizing personal warmth, Christian experience of everyday living, and the building up of Christian virtues. His "little churches" within the church successfully taught self-discipline, including abstinence from card-playing, dancing, and the theatre. Similar proscriptions found their ways into Puritan churches of the British Isles.

Despite charges of heresy, Pietism held fast, and the University of Halle became its chief center. The warm heart and social concern of

Pietism at Halle inspired the commission of missionaries to India, and at least one, a Lutheran, Henry Melchior Muhlenberg, to Germans in the American colonies.

Although the churches had been protected by the *Treaties of Westphalia*, they were isolated from one another in a divided Germany. Neither peace treaties nor the warming of hearts to social concern could erase the ravages of war. The population of Germany had been reduced from 16 million' to six million. For lack of manpower, a third of German land still lay fallow between 1648 and 1680. Peasants existed on linseed and oilcakes or bread of bran and moss.

The 17th century was marked by greedy rulers bent on a lifestyle of opulent ease and aggressive attacks on neighboring states. German princes coined money and levied taxes on impoverished people to support it all. In small bands, thousands of German Reformed people, free in their faith in God, quietly slipped away in 1709, to find a haven in London. From there, most sought a permanent home among the American colonists in the New World. Having endured such pain and hardship, many found great promise in the ideal of brotherly love and joined William Penn's Pennsylvania Colony. Others, many of them indentured servants, went to New York, Virginia, and the colonies of North and South Carolina.

THE REFORMATION IN ENGLAND

Reformation ferment crossed the English Channel within 15 years of its outbreak in Europe. In 1534, King Henry VIII (1491–1547) of England, for personal reasons, broke with the Church of Rome and established the Church of England, with himself as its secular head. He appointed an Archbishop of Canterbury as its spiritual leader. England moved beyond permanent Roman Catholic control, although much of the Catholic liturgy and governance by bishops was adopted into the tradition of the Anglican Church (Episcopal, in America). Nevertheless, Lutheran and Reformed theology invaded Anglicanism during the short reign of Henry's son, Edward VI (1547–53), through Archbishop Thomas Cranmer's *Book of Common Prayer*.

Catholic Mary Tudor (1553–58) on becoming Queen of England,

persecuted those who refused to abandon Protestantism and burned Anglican bishops, including Cranmer. Over 800 dissenters fled to the Continent and came under the tutelage of more radical reformers, especially John Calvin. Mary's half-sister, Queen Elizabeth I (1558–1603) succeeded Mary and re-established a more inclusive and tolerant Anglican Church. She warily welcomed from Europe the dissenters, who had become steeped in Reformed theology.

On their return, they joined others who felt that Elizabeth's reformation had not gone far enough. They sought to purify the church. The Puritans, so named in 1563, criticized Anglican liturgy, ceremonies, and lack of discipline, especially of the clergy. Their thrust toward independent thought and church autonomy laid the foundations for Congregationalism. Nevertheless, they remained members of the Church of England.

The Puritans held to Reformed belief in the sovereignty of God, the authority of scripture as the revelation of God's will, and the necessity to bend to the will of God. The Puritans regarded human rituals and institutions as idolatrous impositions upon the word of God. They wanted to rid the church of old remnants of papism. Puritan zeal in spreading their belief about God's confrontation with humanity conflicted sharply with the established church. Nevertheless, the Puritans thought of themselves as members of the church, not founders of new churches.

Elizabeth had no heir, and James I ruled England next (1603–25) and commissioned a new translation of the Bible, known as the *King James Version*. James's Church of England did not satisfy the Puritans. Yet, they could not agree among themselves about their differences with the church. They were called variously, Dissenters, Independents, Non-Conformists or Separatists. By this time, many Puritans were unwilling to wait for Parliament to institute ecclesiastical reform and separated themselves from the Church of England. Among them were groups that later were called Quakers, Baptists, and Congregationalists.

A civil war during the reign of Charles I (1625–49) was led by English and Scottish Puritans who beheaded the king and, under Oliver

Cromwell as Lord Protector, seized English government (1649–60). For 11 years, Puritan radicals ruled England with excessive zeal and the monarchy was restored in 1660.

The "Congregational Way" probably was born in 1567 when a group of Separatists, calling themselves "The Privye Church," worshiped in London's Plumbers' Hall. They were persecuted severely and their leader killed. Clandestine meetings of Congregationalists continued for simple worship in fields and unexpected rooms, dangerously subject to surveillance by spies for the government, who brought persecution upon the worshipers.

Robert Browne, an Anglican priest, was the first conspicuous advocate of Congregationalism in England. By gathering, in 1581, a congregation in Norwich, Brown expressed his conviction that the only true church was a local body of believers who experienced together the Christian life, united to Christ and to one another by a voluntary covenant. Christ, not the king or queen, was the head of such a church; the people were its governors, and would elect a pastor, teacher, elders, and deacons, according to the authority of the New Testament. Further-more, each autonomous church owed communal helpfulness to every other church. Browne was imprisoned 32 times and fled to the Netherlands. Browne retained his beliefs but did not re-main a Congregationalist; he returned from exile in Holland to pastor a small Anglican parish in England.

Among the early Separatists were John Smyth, founder of the Baptist Church, and John Robinson (1573–1625). The lives of both men became entangled with that of William Brewster, who became a leader of the Plymouth Colony in America.

Brewster lent his home at Scrooby Manor as a Separatist meeting place. Richard Clyfton became pastor and John Robinson, teacher. Brewster was ruling elder. In 1607 the Separatist Church was discovered and its members imprisoned, placed under surveillance, or forced to flee. They went first to Amsterdam and then to Leyden, Holland.

Concerned in Leyden that their children were losing touch with English language and culture, and beset by economic problems and threats of war, 102 of the Holland exiles became the Pilgrims who, under John Carver and William Brewster, migrated to the New World, arriving aboard the Mayflower in 1620. As the company left, John Robinson, beloved pastor and teacher who stayed with a majority in Holland, warned the adventurers not to stick fast where Luther and Calvin left them, for he was confident "the Lord has more truth and light yet to break forth out of his Holy Word." Arriving at Plymouth, their leaders realized that the Pilgrims' survival in an unknown, primitive wilderness rested on their remaining loyally together. The Pilgrims drew up and signed the *Association and Agreement*, the Mayflower Compact, thereby forming of the small colony a "Civil Body Politic" for laws and regulations.

In 1630, John Cotton, a brilliant young minister of Boston, Lincolnshire, England, preached a farewell sermon to John Winthrop and his Puritan followers. Cotton reassured them of their clear call from God to follow Congregational principles, but insisted that they need not separate themselves from the Anglican Church. These Puritan emigrants set sail for Massachusetts Bay. At about the same time, a covenanting Puritan colony arrived in America from England under John Endecott to establish its church in Salem, across Massachusetts Bay, north of Boston. They sent a letter to the Separatist Church at Plymouth to ask for guidance. Commissioned delegates from Plymouth extended to the Salem Church "the right hand of fellowship" and so added fellowship in Christ to English Congregationalism's freedom in Christ.

Concerned that there be educated leaders, the Massachusetts Bay Colony voted in 1636 to give £400 to establish a college in Newtowne (Cambridge). Colonist and pastor John Harvard contributed his library and two years later left the institution half his fortune. The college was, and is, called by his name.

CONGREGATIONALISM

Congregations determined the politics and social organization of communities. Only church members could vote at town meetings, and until 1630, one could become a church member only by the minister's endorsement. Most colonists were not church members. The majority of immigrants came for social, political, and economic reasons, not to found a more perfect Christian society. Nevertheless, Puritanism was dominant. Biblical injunctions were specific guides for spiritual life and church organization; biblical law was common law. Puritans undertook a holy mission to demonstrate the "right way" to order church and society.

John Cotton (1584–1652), considered the leading Puritan pastor in England, joined the Massachusetts Bay Colony in 1633. His *True Constitution of a Particular Visible Church*, describing Congregational life and polity (organization and government), was read widely in England and influenced John Owen, chaplain to Oliver Cromwell, to embrace Congregationalism. As a result of reading Cotton's work, five members of the Presbyterian Westminster Assembly, "the Dissenting Brethren," would sign, in 1643, what was to become the manifesto of all Congregationalism, *An Apologeticall Narration*. Thus, through Cotton's writing, New England affected the growth of Congregationalism in England. Quite the opposite of the vigorous and variable Puritans of England, many of the American Puritans become intolerant of alien ideas.

In 1634, Anne Hutchinson, daughter of a nonconformist minister from north of London, arrived. Described by critics as a "woman of haughty and fierce carriage ... of voluble tongue," she would influence Congregational practice and theological thought, such that the rigidly righteous shell of Massachusetts Puritanism, already damaged by Roger Williams (soon banished to Rhode Island), would be irreparably cracked. Opposing a doctrine of the elect, she held that anyone might receive the truth by direct revelation from God, and that the Bible was not its sole source. These ideas were greatly feared by the church because they easily could lead to irresponsible excesses. This "woman of ready wit and bold spirit," wife of gentle William Hutchinson, the mother of fifteen children, interrupted preachers with whom she disagreed. She gathered women regularly in her own home, where she preached to as many as 50 people at a time, often including men.

Hutchinson's criticism of Puritan sermons stirred up a frenzy of concern in Massachusetts Bay Colony. John Cotton, sent to stop her, merely warned her; but by that time, men of stature had taken her side, and the town of Boston was divided. John Winthrop believed that if Anne Hutchinson could not be reformed, she must be exiled.

Winthrop called a Synod of the Bay Colony churches in 1637, that once and for all "the breeder and nourisher of all these distempers, one Mistress Hutchinson," be silenced. She was charged with joining a seditious faction, holding conspiracies in her house, seducing honest people from their work and families and, worst of all, breaking the fifth commandment. Hutchinson exclaimed that Winthrop was neither her father nor her mother, to which Winthrop replied that "father and mother" meant anyone in authority. In the spring, John Cotton betrayed her trust by banishing her from the Colony. Mary Dyer was a friend who walked beside her through it all. She was later hanged for her Quaker faith on Boston Common. Anne Hutchinson settled with her children and husband in the Rhode Island Colony of Roger Williams, where laws were passed to ensure jury trials, to end class discrimination, and to extend universal suffrage and religious tolerance. This democracy was short-lived, for Rhode Island was soon annexed to the Bay Colony.

The colonists displaced Native Americans and invaded their ancestral territories. At first, because of their nature and because land was abundant, many Indians received the newcomers with charity and shared with them land and survival skills. Later, the proprietary aggression of some settlers kindled fear in the hearts of Indians.

The colonists brought not only their religion, government, and social patterns, but also diseases against which Indians had little or no immunity. During the 17th century, New England Indians were plagued by a smallpox epidemic. There followed further decimation of their numbers in wars and skirmishes for possession of land. Distressed by wanton disregard for human beings, convinced that their mission was peacefully to carry the good news of Christ to their Indian neighbors, there were others like John Eliot, who was ordained as a pastor so that he might pastor and teach Indians. His concern for Indian neighbors was not only for their conversion to Christianity, but to raise their standard of living to a level enjoyed by the settlers. For 30 years, Job

Nesutan, a Massachusetts Indian, was employed by Eliot as a language tutor and chief assistant in the ministry to Indians. The Massachusetts language of the Algonquian nation and Indians were taught to read.

By 1646, John Eliot drew increasingly large congregations each time he spoke. Churches in the colony were encouraged to support Eliot's work and Oliver Cromwell urged Parliament to help the movement financially. The "Corporation for the Promoting and Propagating of the Gospel of Jesus Christ in New England" was the result. A sum of £5,000 was sent to the colonies, much of this given to John Eliot for his work. Many Indian converts returned to the practices of their indigenous faiths, but others were filled with Christian missionary zeal and prepared the way for Eliot with the New England tribes. The chiefs and councils tried to discourage the spread of the gospel, and his aides used underhanded tactics to retain "converts." As a result, Eliot's work suffered. Finally, the Massachusetts General Court passed a law prohibiting the use of threats or force to ensure Indians' conversion to Christianity, but at the same time, required all Indians living within the colony to refrain from worshiping "false gods" and from conducting native religious services. Roger Williams became the advocate of Indian freedom to worship as they saw fit.

Thomas Mayhew and his clergyman son, Thomas, Jr., were instrumental in leading the eastern Cape Cod Indians to Christianity. By 1652, Mayhew had opened a school for Indian children.

Christian theology induced ferment and continued to challenge the essentially closed social patterns and purposes of the Puritans. There were blacks in Boston as soon as there were whites, and slavery was legal in New England until after the Revolutionary War. A certain number of blacks were admitted to membership in the churches when they were able to meet all the conditions for full communion, tests which did not include skin color, wealth, or social status. While slavery in New England had been dying out in the years prior to the Revolution, blacks felt keenly the reservations to their acceptance in the churches by the Puritans, who treated them as slaves outside the church, while within, members were called upon to regard one another as equal under the covenant of grace and united by God to one another. Under such ambivalence, many blacks withdrew from the churches in the late 18th century to form their own congregations for separate worship.

By 1789, the Boston selectmen allowed blacks to use a school for public worship on Sunday afternoons. Eventually, the black congregation built its own church, called the African Church, on the back slope of Beacon Hill and worshiped there from 1806 until mid-century when it became a center for abolitionist meetings for blacks and whites. Harriet Tubman, Frederick Douglass and Sojourner Truth were among the speakers at the church.

Religious exclusion was not confined to blacks or Catholics; Presbyterians had felt unwelcome as well. The *Westminster Confession* of 1646, the design for Presbyterian church government and an expression of Reformed faith and doctrine, was revised for church polity and discipline at the Cambridge Synod of 1648. Called the *Cambridge Platform*, it enabled a reconciliation between Presbyterians and Congregationalists and was highly venerated into the 19th century.

The *Platform* interpreted the church catholic as all those who are elected and called to salvation. A "militant visible church on earth" was understood to exist in particular congregations as "a company of saints by calling, united into one body, by a holy covenant for the public worship of God and the mutual edification of one another." Christ was head of the church; the congregation, independent of outside interference, had the right to choose its own officials. The office of the civil magistrate was subject to recognition by the church. Churches were to preserve communion with one another in mutual covenant with Christ. Such covenants stabilized churches establishing themselves under disparate leadership.

A remarkable succession of educated clergy provided strong leadership. Despite the circumstances that cast him in the role of villain in the excommunication and banishment of Anne Hutchinson, no Puritan teacher was more respected in England and in America than the gentle intellectual, John Cotton, minister of First Church, Boston. His colleague from days in England was the plain-spoken master of rhythmic rhetoric and the effective metaphor, Thomas Hooker (1586–1647).

Hooker, committed to democracy and constitutional free government, was minister across the Charles River at Newtowne (Cambridge).

Concerned for human rights, Hooker became disenchanted with the elitism of the Boston hierarchy. He led over 100 followers to migrate on foot to Hartford in 1636. There, buoyed by his Christian conviction and liberating ideas of democracy, he established a colony. Conservative Puritan minister, John Davenport, founder of the New Haven Colony, was so offended by Hooker's willingness to secularize, even to a limited extent, civil government, that he went to Boston when New Haven was gathered into the Connecticut Colony.

All these men were well educated, had high standards for church membership, and were clergy of the English establishment. Except for Cotton, their Reformed covenant theology had been nurtured on the continent. Hooker, who had been with the dissenters in Holland, diverged from the orthodox Puritan view that voting rights should be conferred only with church membership. He saw no justice in disenfranchising nine-tenths of the population, a proportion which included women, children, servants and apprentices, the unchurched who had migrated from England as non-land owners, as well as the sons of "the elect" who could not pretend to such a claim.

Under Hooker's leadership, the Connecticut Colony gave up the religious qualification for the franchise. New requirements were still restrictive. They gave the town meeting vote to "admitted inhabitants," "men" who could prove capable of "an honest conversation" and could swear that they were not "a Jew, a Quaker or an Atheist," and to "free men who were Trinitarians, land owners and of godly deportment." Nevertheless, Hooker is regarded by many as the father of democracy in America, for many of his ideas were embodied in the United States Constitution.

Later, Massachusetts adopted the controversial Half-Way Covenant of 1662, permitting children to be baptized whose grandparents had been members of the church, but whose parents were not. Males baptized under the Covenant could vote at town meeting when they came of age, but were not admitted to the Lord's Supper or allowed to vote for a pastor. Full church membership came with confession of faith. Its requirement to sit in judgment upon a person's Christian credentials would go to the extreme of the witchcraft delusion in Salem Village by 1692.

Later, Cotton Mather (1663–1728), John Cotton's grandson, sought to bring some authority to bear upon the waywardness of Congregational independence. He proposed that ministers in association with one another examine and license candidates for the ministry, and that a consociation of ministers and lay-men have judicatory standing over the churches. A minister unpopular among his peers, Mather's proposal was at first unacceptable. In 1705–6, Massachusetts finally adopted his plan for the examination of ministers. Connecticut issued the *Saybrook Platform* in 1708, making both of Mather's proposals binding colonywide. The establishment in 1701 of Yale College assured high educational standards for ministers and leaders alike.

Until the *Saybrook Platform* of 1708, upheld by the Connecticut General Court, imposed upon the independent, voluntary fellowship of the churches an obligation of "consociation," the Congregationalists drifted toward spiritual decline and anomaly. The consociation provided mutual aid and outside assistance in handling disputes. A penalty was provided for churches or pastors refusing consociation, a "sentence of non-communion," with less intent to control than to provide orderly procedures and mutual support. The new shape would enable Congregationalism as a denomination in the centuries to come, to maintain its integrity in the face of the American Revolution, religious revivals, the scandal of slavery, the challenge of cultural pluralism, and a call to mission that would carry the faith west-ward and world-wide.

The morality of Pietism, and the warm heart of England's Wesleyan revival that gave birth to the Methodist Church, helped to energize the American Great Awakening. Itinerant preachers of various denominations swept across religious America during the mid-18th century, winning Christian converts and planting hundreds of new churches. While the Coetus of Pennsylvania was giving nurture and support to a continuing influx of German settlers, over 150 new Congregational churches were formed from 1740 to 1760.

Yale-educated Jonathan Edwards (1703–58) of Northampton, Massachusetts, Congregational minister of keen philosophical intellect, believed that the Awakening was breathing new life into the churches. It replaced a view of the church as a group of people who covenanted together to lead a Christian life, with one that insisted upon individual conversion as the accepted way to the kingdom of God. Emotions ran high, and the spiritual climates that had in many communities fallen into despair, were transformed.

In 1750, Edwards was dismissed from the Northampton church. He tangled with the congregation on issues of church discipline and tact. For example, he read the names of both the convicted and merely indicted ("bad book controversy") aloud in church as a single list. The final issue surrounded a difference in his interpretation of the Half-Way Covenant (he rejected it as too lax a standard of church membership) from that of his grandfather, Solomon Stoddard, whose associate Edwards had first been at Northampton. Edwards was convinced that admission to communion should include the requirement of a conversion experience. Although a strict Calvinist, Jonathan Edwards had become a "New Light" revivalist Puritan sympathizer. He disagreed with the narrow conservatism of the "Old Light" ministers such as Increase Mather and his son, Cotton, and stood firmly against liberal "Arminians," whose moral righteousness he saw as dangerously smug. Nevertheless, he believed that turning to God required a decision, a disavowal of selfishness and the adoption of the life of "disinterested benevolence." Edwards was joined in his position by a large group of New England clergy who supported the Awakening and opposed the more staid, rational, liberal movement in eastern Massachusetts. A group of moderates stood between both extremes. The Boston advocates of free will against Calvinism opposed the revivals, and the path they took would lead in the next century to the Unitarian separation from Congregationalism.

Jonathan Edwards, foremost of American philosophers, was responsible for a far broader synthesis of science, philosophy, and religion in Congregational and Presbyterian theology and practice than had been present in "Old Light" Puritanism. He integrated with Reformed theology the world view of Isaac Newton, John Locke's emphasis upon human experience, and Augustine's spiritual enlightenment, as well as Plato's idealism and the Neo-Platonic idea of emanation from the Divine Intellect to the soul. His ideas would cohere in his followers to give life to a "New England Theology." They would check the anti-intellectual tendencies of the revivalists and the decline of religious vitality during the Revolutionary period. They would give a theological framework to the recovery of intellectual leadership and a new morality in post-Revolutionary America. Edwards' writings inspired and informed the missionary movement of the 19th century as America expanded westward and looked once again to the lands across the sea. His influence rivaled Hooker's in developing the separation of church and state.

THE GERMAN REFORMED CHURCH

While the independent Congregationalists had been struggling in New England to recover and maintain biblical faithfulness, a stream of German and German-Swiss settlers—farmers, laborers, trade and craftpersons, many "redemptioners" who had sold their future time and services to pay for passage—flowed into Pennsylvania and the Middle Atlantic region. Refugees from the waste of European wars, their concerns were pragmatic. They did not bring pastors with them. People of Reformed biblical faith, at first sustained only by family worship at home, they were informed by the Bible and the *Heidelberg Catechism*.

Strong relationships developed between Lutheran and Reformed congregations; many union churches shared buildings. At first, there were no buildings and laymen often led worship. In 1710, a Dutch Reformed minister, Paul Van Vlecq, assisted a German congregation gathered at Skippack, Pennsylvania. At nearby White Marsh, Van Vlecq established a congregation in the house of elder William Dewees, who held the congregation together until the church was reestablished in 1725.

Another layman, tailor Conrad Templeman, conducted services in Lancaster county, ministering to seven congregations during the 1720s. Schoolmaster John Philip Boehm had maintained a ministry for five years without compensation. Responsible for the regular organization of 12 German Reformed congregations in Pennsylvania, although not regularly ordained, he reluctantly was persuaded to celebrate the sacraments for the first time on October 15, 1725, at Falkner Swamp, with 40 members present. Boehm, orderly, well educated, devout, spent the ensuing years traveling the country on horseback, 25, 000 miles in all, preparing Reformed Church constitutions.

Meanwhile, the Heidelberg-educated and regularly ordained pastor George Michael Weiss arrived from Germany in 1727 to minister to the Philadelphia church founded by Boehm. He carried the Word and the Lord's Supper to communities surrounding Philadelphia. Weiss' strong objections to Boehm's irregular ministry caused Boehm to seek and receive ordination by the Dutch Reformed Church by 1729. Funds for American churches were still coming from Europe, and Weiss went abroad to Holland in pursuit of support for his congregations. Successful, he returned in 1731 to minister among German Reformed people in New York.

Before 1746, when Michael Schlatter, a Swiss-born and Dutch-educated young pastor from Heidelberg, arrived in America, congregations of German settlers were scattered throughout Pennsylvania and New York. German immigrants had followed natural routes along rivers and mountain valleys, and Reformed congregations had emerged in Maryland, Virginia, and North Carolina. The spiritual and financial health of these 40 congregations was watched over by the Dutch Reformed Church in Holland, assisted by the German Reformed center at Heidelberg, Germany.

Support came from the Classis ("association") of Amsterdam that sent Michael Schlatter to America to "organize the ministers and congregations into a Coetus (synod)." Schlatter did this within a year of his arrival in Pennsylvania. With the cooperation of Boehm, Weiss, John Bartholomew Rieger, and 28 elders, the Coetus of the Reformed Ministerium of the Congregations in Pennsylvania came to life on September 24, 1747 and the Coetus adopted in 1748 the *Kirchen-Ordnung* that Boehm had prepared in 1725. The *Kirchen-Ordnung* placed discipline and care of the local church in the hands of a consistory of elders, deacons, and the minister, elected by the congregation. Members were charged with "fraternal correction and mutual edification." The minister was to preach "the pure doctrine of the Reformed Church according to the Word of God and to administer the holy seals of the Covenant ... : always to adhere to the Heidelberg Catechism ... to hold catechetical instruction ... [and] give special attention to church discipline, together with those who have oversight of the congregation."

In light of the multiplicity of German sects, such as Moravians, Mennonites and Dunkards, who competed for the attention and allegiance of German immigrants, the authority of the Coetus, organized according to the same structure and discipline as the local church, was welcome. The German Reformed Churches felt protected from "unscrupulous proselitizers." They achieved a mutual identity and respect, and established authority for faith and practice. Among pastor and people, shared responsibility was carried out within a community of faith, under the Lordship of Christ. The leadership of Michael Schlatter and his colleagues prepared the congregations to endure the upheaval of the American Revolution and to maintain their identity in the ethnic and religious pluralism that characterized William Penn's colony.

Many German Reformed settlers served in the Revolutionary armies, 20 percent of Reformed pastors as chaplains, although Continental Congress Chaplain John Joachim Zubly was labeled a Tory for his anti-war stand. During the British siege of Philadelphia in 1777, farmers wrapped the Liberty Bell and the bells of Christ Church in potato sacks and hauled them to Allentown, Pennsylvania, where pastor Abraham Blumer hid them under the floor of Zion Reformed Church for safekeeping. Friedrich Wilhelm von Steuben, a Reformed layman, disciplined Washington's troops during the bitter Valley Forge winter.

The Coetus strengthened the churches and prepared them for self-government in the early years of the United States. By 1793, European ties were broken. A Reformed Church Constitution was adopted, a *Synodal Ordnung*; an official name was taken, The Synod of the German Reformed Church in the United States of America, and a hymnbook committee appointed. There were in that year, 178 German-speaking congregations and 15,000 communicant members.

Revival theology was antithetical to the German Reformed tradition. However, pietistic influences within the German Reformed Church responded to the warm-hearted moral virtue of the revival. On the frontier, people found its emphasis on the individual compatible with their needs. The newly independent German Reformed Church, short of pastors and threatened by a revivalist gospel, established a seminary in 1825, at Carlisle, Pennsylvania, that moved in 1829 to York, in 1837 to Mercersburg and finally to Lancaster in 1871, where it became Lancaster Theological Seminary. Franklin College (1787) of Lancaster, jointly supported by the Lutherans and the Reformed, in 1853 merged with German Reformed Marshall College to form Franklin and Marshall College.

As ministers arrived in America from the pietist centers in Europe, pietistic rather than confessional patterns appeared in Reformed congregations, and the guiding light of the catechism was dimmed. Missionary zeal abounded. People were highly susceptible to the leadership of charismatic frontier preachers. Church leaders were concerned that young and old be instructed in Reformed Christian doctrine. In 1806, the first German Reformed Sunday schools appeared. In the midst of it all, and in reaction to revivalist sectarianism, a controversial movement at the seminary at Mercersburg set off a re-examination of the doctrines of Christ and of the church not just in the German Reformed Church but among all American Protestants.

First, however, there would be years of ferment when the Synod would endure turmoil and defection that would test and eventually strengthen its essential stability. Pietist minister Philip William Otterbein, a Reformed Church pastor, later founded the United Brethren Church, today a part of the United Methodist Church. Harrisburg's pastor, John Winebrenner, locked out of his church by the consistory, met with his followers in private homes to form a new denomination, The Churches of God.

As the Reformed Church grew, continuing use of the German language became an issue. Although German congregations were divided between the use of German or English, the Synod itself conducted meetings and issued minutes in German until 1825. By 1824, the Ohio

Synod separated from the parent synod in order to ordain its own ministers and in 1850 organized Heidelberg College and Seminary in Tiffin.

The controversial Mercersburg movement would shake the church. With the arrival at the Mercersburg seminary of John W. Nevin and Swiss-German professor of historical and exegetical theology, Philip Schaff, Mercersburg became a center of concern that the revivalism of the Awakening was inauthentic. Schaff was the most outstanding church historian in 19th-century America and the primary mediator of German theology to America.

The Mercersburg movement, counter to the sectarian trend of the time, called for a "true revival" centered in the life of the church, guided by the catechetical system, and in particular, the *Heidelberg Catechism*. The movement's leaders called for a recognition of the church as one, catholic, and holy. They acknowledged the error to which the church in all ages had been subject, urged an end to sectarianism and pretensions to the one true church and called for cessation of anti-Catholicism which had been pervasive for some time. Schaff's charitable attitude was seen by some in the Philadelphia Classis, the "Old Reformed" and loyal to Zwingli's Reformation, as heresy. Nevin, Schaff, and their followers sought to go back to the creeds and to make the mystical presence of Christ, mediated by word and sacrament, the essence of the church. Reverence for the creeds, catechism, and liturgy, they believed, would unify the church and combat sectarianism. In liturgy, the Mercersburg people favored an altar as the center for worship with formal litanies, chants, prayers and clerical garb, while "Old Reformed" pastors preferred a central pulpit, free prayer and informal worship.

The "Old Reformed" were caught up in the American revival and clung to their German sectarian identities. Schaff maintained that Reformed theology's contribution to the New World lay in the supremacy of the scriptures, absolute sovereignty of divine grace, and radical moral reform on the basis of both. A former member of The Evangelical Church of The Prussian Union, Schaff later cultivated warm relationships with Evangelicals in the West.

The Mercersburg Review, the movement's chief literary medium, which began publication at Marshall College in 1848, was greatly responsible for effecting changed attitudes. Its challenge would call other denominations to self-examination as well. It was the German Reformed Church's initial contribution to the movement toward unity and ecumenism that would take shape in the next century.

The low church "Old Reformed" minority in the East, after a long struggle against a revised liturgy, called a convention in Myerstown, Pennsylvania in 1867 to prevent its use. In January, 1868, the *Reformed Church Quarterly* began and in 1870, Ursinus College opened its doors, supported by the "Old Reformed."

EDUCATION AND MISSION

The rise of denominationalism in the 19th century was a phenomenon for which Congregational churches, independent although loosely associated, were ill prepared. Rejecting anything that smacked of centralized authority, the churches contained no efficient mechanism for corporate action or cohesive principle around which to organize corporately. They were churches, not Church.

No single event was responsible for the movement toward state and national levels of organization and communion. Rather, a positive and vigorous reappraisal of Congregational history provided a powerful emotional undergirding for a newly articulated American denomination. In the democratic tendencies of their polity, Congregationalists discovered a remarkable affinity with the emergent American nationalism. The polity that allowed for diversity appeared to be an ecclesiastical counterpart to the democratic polity of the nation itself. They rediscovered Cotton Mather's unity in diversity and by 1871 a new, corporate identity was asserted. Their unity lay in a commitment to the diversity produced and embraced by the polity itself—a commitment continued in the United Church of Christ.

An atmosphere of political and religious liberty spawned American denominationalism. Each denomination began new educational institutions. Before William Ellery Channing, Congregational minister in Boston, had proclaimed his leadership of the Unitarian movement by preaching in 1819 his famous sermon, "Unitarian Christianity," the liberal professor of divinity at Harvard, Henry Ware, set off a controversy that sparked the establishment of the Congregational Andover Theological Seminary in 1808, a bulwark of Calvinist orthodoxy.

Andover was instrumental in preparing the first Congregational missionaries for overseas mission. The churches already had sent missionaries to frontier America. The American overseas missionary movement had its informal beginning in 1806 when Samuel J. Mills met with four fellow students at Williams College in Massachusetts for a Sunday afternoon prayer meeting in a maple grove. A sudden thunderstorm drove them to the shelter of a haystack where amidst the thunderclaps and flashes of lightning, Mills proposed sending the gospel to Asia. His zeal ignited the four others with the intent "to evangelize the world," and they went on to study theology at Andover Seminary. Together, they confirmed their purpose and maintained their association throughout their theological studies.

One of them, Adoniram Judson, who later became a Baptist, had appealed to the London Missionary Society for support and had been rejected. Feeling that it was time for American Congregationalism to support its own missionaries, the Andover faculty and leaders of the Massachusetts General Association authorized a joint missionary venture by the churches of Massachusetts and Connecticut. On September 5, 1810, the American Board of Commissioners for Foreign Missions was born. On February 8, 1812, at a moving service of worship in a crowded Salem Tabernacle Church, the Haystack "Brethren" were ordained. Within two weeks, they set sail for India.

In the same year, New England Congregational clergy brought nearly unanimous condemnation on the War of 1812 as "unnecessary, unjust, and inexpedient." Their regular anti-war sermons and constituency organizing in opposition to government policy were unprecedented as a united ministerial action. Nevertheless, on June 20, 1812, a charter was granted the American Board of Commissioners for Foreign Missions to serve the Congregational churches as their agent for foreign mission, the first foreign missionary society in America.

The German Reformed Church Synod in 1826 voted to establish

an American Missionary Society of the Reformed Church "to promote the interests of the church within the United States and elsewhere." The German Reformed Church recognized that a single board could best serve all abroad, and John W. Nevin was appointed to represent the church on the American Board. By 1866, when the German Reformed Church withdrew to manage its own mission, all other denominations represented on the board had done the same.

The American Board of Commissioners for Foreign Missions had intended to establish missions not only in the Orient and Burma, but also "in the West among the Iroquois." Subsequently, throughout the 1820s and 1830s missions were established among the Creek, Choctaw, Chickasaw and Cherokee, Osage, Maumee and Iroquois. In an interdenominational effort, members of the American Board supported and aided Indian resistance to government removal from their lands.

In a celebrated case, the American Board backed Samuel A. Worcester, missionary to the Cherokee, in his United States Supreme Court suit against the state of Georgia in 1830, to sustain Cherokee sovereignty over their land. Although the court ruled that the Cherokee nation was under United States protection and could not be removed by Georgia, President Andrew Jackson had the tribes removed anyway. Outrage at injustice toward Native Americans called out and dispersed many missionaries to tribes throughout the United States.

Later in the 19th century, the German Reformed Church initiated missions to new German settlers and nearby Indian settlements. More than 300 churches were constructed.

Swiss and German students at Mercersburg Theological Seminary aided Germans on the western frontier. With the initial purpose of training local men as ministers and teachers, the Sheboygan Classis of the Wisconsin Synod established Mission House in 1862. Started as an academy, it soon became a college (1879) and seminary (1880). In 1957, Mission House College became Lakeland College and Mission House Seminary merged with the Congregational Christian Yankton School of Theology in 1962 to become the United Theological Seminary of the Twin Cities at New Brighton, Minnesota.

Mission House initiated an Indian ministry in the 1870s by an act of providence. Professor H. Kurtz, overtaken by a snow-storm, succumbed to fatigue on a 12-mile return walk from a Sunday preaching mission. Some Winnebagos, finding him asleep and in danger of freezing, took him home to Mission House. Naturally, Kurtz promoted help for Indians of the area, and in 1876, the Classis declared, "As soon as we have the money to find a missionary, we will send him to the Indians who live nearest us." Jacob Hauser was sent in 1878 and was warily received, but concern for their children's education and the basic affirmation that all shared one God, the Earthmaker, allowed the Winnebago to accept the basic ministry of the Hausers. Twenty years later a church was started. In 1917, a boarding school opened that became the Winnebago Indian School at Neillsville, Wisconsin. The school provided Christian ministers, teachers, nurses, and leaders for the tribe, among them Mitchell Whiterabbit, a pastor who became a national leader in the United Church of Christ.

The 18th-century Great Awakening had been unconcerned with sectarian labels. Under the *Plan of Union* (1801) and the Accommodation Plan (1808), the theologically compatible Congregational and Presbyterian churches cooperated in their missionary efforts in the West. A minister of either denomination might be chosen by a congregation that was functioning under the polity of its founding denomination. Under the Accommodation Plan, Congregational Associations were received by Presbyterian Synods until 1837 when self-conscious denominationalism caused Presbyterians to withdraw. Congregationalists followed suit in 1852 when the Congregational churches were united into a national organization for the first time.

The first New England Congregational colony in the Northwest Territory was established at Marietta, Ohio, in 1788. Education a primary value, Muskingum Academy was soon opened and in 1835 became Marietta College. Congregationalists and Presbyterians planted colleges along the way. Most of the early colleges, including Harvard, Yale, and Princeton long ago declared independence of a denominational connection. Thirteen frontier colleges have affirmed their diverse historical denominational ties with the United Church of Christ. Beloit (1846) received its roots from the Presbyterian and Congregational Churches. The others are Illinois (1829), Olivet (1844), Grinnell (1846), Pacific (1849), Ripon (1851), Carleton (1866), Doane (1872), Drury (1873), Westminster (1875), Yankton (1881), Rocky Mountain (1883) and Northland (1892). Those with Evangelical, Reformed, and Christian roots that continue to relate through the Council for Higher Education to the United Church of Christ are Franklin and Marshall (1787), Heidelberg (1850), Defiance (1850), Cedar Crest (1867), Ursinus (1869), Elmhurst (1871), Elon (1889), Hood (1893), Lakeland (1893), Hawaii Loa College (1963), and six colleges established in the South after the Civil War, mentioned later in more detail.

The need to train ministers called forth fifteen seminaries related to the denominations that formed the United Church of Christ. Eight maintain a historic relationship with the church and are members of the Council for Higher Education. They are: Harvard Divinity School (1816), Yale Divinity School (1822), Hartford Seminary (1834), Vanderbilt Divinity School (1875), Seminario Evangelico de Puerto Rico (1919) and Interdenominational Theological Center in Atlanta (1958).

Seven schools rooted in our history are recognized today as seminaries of the United Church of Christ and are members of both the Council for Higher Education and the Council for Theological Education. They are: Andover Newton Theological School (1807), Bangor Theological Seminary (1814), Lancaster Theological Seminary (1825), Eden Theological Seminary (1850), Chicago Theological Seminary (1855), Pacific School of Religion (1866) and United Theological Seminary of the Twin Cities (1962).

In a more open society, women emerged in greater numbers, often at great risk, from the confines of their homes and families to respond to a Christian calling. Congregational educators such as Emma Willard, Catherine Beecher, Sarah Porter, and Mary Lyon, and a writer appalled by the injustice of slavery, Harriet Beecher Stowe, were characterized by persistence. Betsy Stockton, a freed slave, sailed in 1822 from Connecticut with 13 others to aid the first contingent of missionaries to Hawaii, sent by the American Board of Commissioners for Foreign Missions, the Congregational forerunner of the United

Church Board for World Ministries. A gifted and versatile Christian woman, Betsy Stockton taught school, lent her homemaking skills for the use of all, nursed and cared for the Islands' sick.

Although her family discouraged her and Oberlin Theological School denied her the degree she had earned, Antoinette Brown sought for three years a call to pastor a church. A call finally came from the Congregational Church in Butler, New York. There she was ordained in 1853, an ordination recognized only by the local church. Her pastorate was short, for she would soon marry Samuel Blackwell and later give birth to seven daughters. Antoinette Brown's activist stand persisted for the abolition of slavery, for the promotion of temperance, and for the establishment of biblical support for equality between women and men. She wrote nine books and in 1920, at age 95, cast her first vote. By 1921, the year of her death, there were 3,000 women ministers in the United States. Her ordination itself had major implications. Her life and ministry are memorialized at each General Synod of the United Church of Christ when the Antoinette Brown Award is presented to two ordained women whose ministries exemplify her dedication and leadership.

Elvira Yockey, a German Reformed pastor's wife in 1887 founded and became the first president of the Women's Missionary Society of the General Synod. She wrote of her experience at Xenia, Ohio: "Here, as all over the Reformed Church, the women were expected to `keep silence in the churches.' Their voices were never heard even in public prayer, and to this day, in most of the prayer meetings of the church the number of *audible* prayers is limited to the number of men present. How much the church owes to the number of silent prayers that ascend heavenward from feminine hearts, can never be known."[1]

Few women could at first take advantage of higher education, but during the 19th century evangelical reform movement, missionary societies became ways for more women to relate to the public sphere. Still demeaned by female role enforcement, women were permitted only to form auxiliary fundraising units, well out of range of policy making. The Female Cent Society, New England forerunner of the Woman's Society of the Congregational Christian Churches, was such an organization.

The Evangelical Synod's deaconess movement provided an acceptable vehicle for women's active involvement in evangelism and social service. Through periodicals, study circles, and organizations, women shared moral issues of the time. Countless volunteer hours were given by women to the alleviation of social ills as the earliest Sunday school teachers, as abolitionists, preachers, teachers, nurses, missionaries, and activists for their own liberation as children of God.

The end of the Civil War freed the hearts and imaginations of Protestants to again envision a revitalized Christianity in America. Congregationalist minister Horace Bushnell led with a vision of a virtuous, joyous, worshiping nation, a Christian commonwealth preserving the separation of church and state that would set the pace for others in the world. Other Congregationalists also were prominent. Bushnell's disciple Josiah Strong sought to rally concerned social action for the urban blight of growing industrialization. Columbus, Ohio minister Washington Gladden, father of the social gospel, defended the right of labor to organize. Jane Addams saw the urgency of the urban poor and began Hull House, the Chicago settlement house, in 1889.

The many voluntary church societies responded to humanitarian concerns aroused by the religious awakenings. The American Home Missionary Society (1826) touched fingertips with the German churches by providing funds for the religious and educational needs of settlers in the West. In 1927, the Iowa-born General Conference of German Congregational Churches was recognized by the General Council along with other Congregational Churches.

The American Missionary Association believed in the transforming power of the gospel to right social evils, particularly inhumanity to other races and the injustice of slavery. The AMA, founded in 1846 as the continuation of the Amistad Committee of 1839, that fought for the release of the African Mendi captives abroad the Amistad ship was by charter, committed to "an elimination of caste." Black and white Americans were active supporters and workers. Engaged from its inception in abolitionist activity, the affirmation of Indian rights, and work among the Eskimo, the AMA responded immediately following the Civil War to the educational and religious needs of freed blacks in the South and of Native Americans. A shortage of educators turned the Association to the education of teachers, and the black colleges were born. A relationship with the United Church of Christ would continue to be maintained by Fisk (1866), Talladega (1867), LeMoyne-Owen (1871), Huston-Tillotson (1876), Dillard (1869) and Tougaloo (1869).

The legal autonomy of the voluntary missionary societies left the Congregational churches and the legislative General Council without administrative authority over the direction of their own mission. The relationship bred long periods of unease. A partial solution came in 1917 when representative voting members of the Council were made voting members of the societies. Corporate law gave final control to boards and directors. Gradually, the home mission and education societies found it expedient to unite under the Board of Home Missions.

The Synod of the German Reformed Church had responded to needs of the people on the frontier by establishing, in 1819, a missionary committee that in 1865 became the Board of Home Missions. In 1866, the German Reformed Church decided not to unite with the Dutch Reformed Church. Dropping the "German" from its name, the church became in 1867, the Reformed Church in the United States.

Responsibility for home mission in the Reformed Church fell to the regional Synods. They were reluctant to comply when the 1878 General Synod resolved that "all home missions of the church should be brought under direct control of the General Synod's board as speedily as possible." When synods finally relinquished control of their mission programs, centralization allowed for productive overall planning and projects such as homes for children and the aged, assistance to Hungarian congregations, new church development, and (after the merger with the Evangelical Synod) work during World War II among Japanese-Americans placed in American concentration camps. Henry Tani, first director of youth ministry in the United Church of Christ, was a layman reached by the last ministry.

The Christian Churches

Of all the United Church of Christ traditions, the Christian Churches were most uniquely American in origin and character. In

Virginia, Vermont, and Kentucky, the Second Great Awakening in the early 1800s stirred the hearts of quite disparate leaders and their followers with the impulse to return to the simplicity of early Christianity. The first group was gathered in 1794 in Virginia by a Revolutionary soldier, James O'Kelley. He, with many other Methodists left the church over their objection to bishops. Methodism, they felt, was too autocratical. They wanted the frontier churches to be freed to deal with the needs and concerns that were different from those of the more established churches. They declared that the Bible was their only guide and adopted as their new name, the Christian Church.

A few years later, at Lyndon, Vermont, Abner Jones and his followers objected to Calvinist Baptist views. In 1801, they organized the First Free Christian Church, in which Christian character would be the only requirement for membership, and in which all who could do so in faith, were welcome to partake of the Lord's Supper. Christ was seen to be more generous than to withhold Communion from all but those who had been baptized by immersion. Jones was later joined by Baptist Elias Smith, who helped to organize a Christian church in Portsmouth, New Hampshire, and began publishing, in 1808, the *Herald of Gospel Liberty*. Smith's paper became a means of drawing the separate Christian movements together.

With a minimum of organization, other churches of like mind were established and the movement became known as the "Christian Connection." The "Connection" had been organized in 1820 at the first United General Conference of Christians, during which six principles were unanimously affirmed:

1. Christ, the only head of the Church.
2. The Bible, sufficient rule of faith and practice.
3. Christian character, the only measurement for membership.
4. The right of private judgment, interpretation of scripture, and liberty of conscience.
5. The name "Christian," worthy for Christ's followers.
6. Unity of all Christ's followers in behalf of the world.

By 1845, a regional New England Convention began.

A third group, under Barton W. Stone, withdrew in 1803 from the

Presbyterian Synod of Kentucky in opposition to Calvinist theology. Stone's followers eventually numbered 8,000 and they, too, took the name Christian. Followers of Stone spread into Ohio, Indiana, and Illinois. Some of this group united with followers of Alexander Campbell at Lexington, Kentucky in 1832 to found the Christian Church (Disciples of Christ) which became the largest indigenous body of Protestants in America. (In the 1970s, the Christian Church [Disciples of Christ] and the United Church of Christ began conversations to consider possible union). Christians who refused to follow Stone and unite with the Disciples, gradually identified with the Christian Churches led by O'Kelley in Virginia and by Jones and Smith in New England.

From 1844, when the New England Convention passed a strong resolution condemning slavery, until long after the Civil War was over, the Christian Churches of the North and the South suspended fellowship with each other. As a result, whites controlled the newly-formed Southern Christian Association. In the North, the first Christian General Convention was held in 1850, and for the first time, Christians began to behave as a denomination.

Christians valued education since their first leaders came from well-educated New England families that had exhibited a humanitarian spirit. In 1844, Christians helped to establish Meadville Seminary with the Unitarians. In 1850, Defiance College in Ohio was born and two years later the coeducational Antioch College, Horace Mann its president, came into being in Ohio. Elon College was founded in North Carolina in 1889, and a year later, the suspended fellowship between northern and southern churches was restored. Christian colleges were recognized as holding the key to an educated clergy and an enlightened church membership.

There was a leveling influence in the frontier church that promoted a democratic spirit. The Great Awakening on the frontier promoted an anti-creedal religion, independent personal judgment, and freedom of conscience. Quite different from the rough nature of frontier life itself, educated leadership brought refined sensibilities, compassion, and concern for humanitarian causes to the churches.

James O'Kelley's denunciation of slavery in 1789 had attracted many blacks to join Christian churches in the South. They were further attracted by the revival style and the zeal for humanitarian reform. Neither race nor gender was a stumbling block to Christian fellowship in the South. Black churches were not organized before the Civil War and in 1852, Isaac Scott, a black man from North Carolina, was ordained by the Christian Church and sent to Liberia as the first overseas missionary from that denomination. The democratic social structure in the Christian Church proved more hospitable to women's sense of "calling" than had been true in Puritan New England churches. In 1839, the Virginia Christian Conference recognized an Ohio minister's wife, the former Rebecca L. Chaney, as her husband's official associate in preaching. The Christian Church exercised its independence under God when it became the first denomination to recognize the ordination of a woman. In 1867, at Ebenezer Church in Clark County, Ohio, Melissa Terrel was ordained to the Christian ministry.

Following the Civil War, black members of the Christian Church tended to cut themselves off from whites to form churches of their own. The black church became the only social structure totally supported by the black community. Elevated to a high status in a climate that denigrated black males, black ministers were close to a peer relationship with white community leaders. Black church ministers were not only pastors and preachers to their congregations, but were social workers and organizers for human rights as well. Black ministers and their churches were often targets of reaction, sometimes violent, during repeated periods of local political battle over issues such as freedom from oppression, the achievement of voting rights, opportunity for land ownership, equality of educational and vocational opportunity, the right to participate in the same amenities offered others in American communities.

Women in many black Christian churches became, to an even greater degree than in white churches, the backbone of church life; many became preachers. Black women so reared, upon joining integrated churches, found it difficult to accept less crucial tasks where men dominated.

The Reconstruction Era after the Civil War was slow and painful. During the time of estrangement, Christian churches of both North and South had increasingly assumed characteristics of a denomination. During the first post-war decade, the Southern Convention adopted a manual for standardized worship and Christian Church rites, as well as for defining "Principles" for Christians. During this period, a group of freed slaves established, in 1866–67, the North Carolina Colored Christian Conference. This group maintained close ties with white Christians and shared in the General Convention of the Christian Church. In 1874, the Eastern Atlantic Colored Christian Conference was formed and in 1873, the Virginia Colored Christian Conference. As numbers of black Christian churches increased, the churches organized themselves further into conferences. In 1892, the Afro-American Convention met for the first time representing five conferences with a total membership of 6,000.

The General Convention of 1874 adopted a *Manifesto*, defining for the Christian Church movement true unity as based not on doctrine or polity, but on Christian spirit and character. The Manifesto stated: "We are ready to form a corporate union with any body of Christians upon the basis of those great doctrines which underlie the religion of Christ ... We are ready to submit all minor matters to ... the individual conscience."

Not until 1890 was the division between the North and the South sufficiently overcome to adopt a *Plan of Union* that formed a new General Convention.

THE GERMAN EVANGELICAL SYNOD

Different from their compatriots who had arrived in America a century earlier, German immigrants between 1830 and 1845 were likely to have lived through the strife inflicted by the Napoleonic wars and a long history of religious coercion by the state. Yet, many Germans were enlightened by rationalist doctrine, art, music, and science. Frederick William III had united the Lutheran and Reformed Churches in 1817 into the Evangelical Church of the Prussian Union. Objections from both church groups would not be countenanced.

Suppression and persecution caused some Lutherans to leave Germany. Traveling by ship and covered wagon, they arrived in Missouri to become the nucleus of the Missouri Synod Lutheran denomination. These conservative people remain "separatist" until the present, still wary of the forced compromises of a coerced union.

Others, both Lutheran and Reformed, embodied the inward and irenic spirit of Pietism as well as its moral missionary zeal. While their leaders were well educated and biblically grounded, they were not attuned to rationalist doctrine or ecclesiastical organization. Enlightened evangelical societies from Basel and Barmen, caring little for confessional distinctions, cooperated with the London Missionary Society and the Church of England to send missionaries abroad.

Between 1830 and 1845, 40,000 people left Germany annually for America where they joined the westward movement. Most settled in Missouri, Illinois, Indiana, Michigan, Iowa and Wisconsin. The German Evangelical Church Society of the West (Der Deutsche Evangelische Kirchenverein des Westens), founded in 1840 at Gravois Settlement, St. Louis, Missouri, was a transplanted Evangelical Church of the Prussian Union.

As with the early Reformed congregations, the Evangelical immigrants were at first pastored by lay people. Although Presbyterians and Congregationalists had tried to welcome them, language was a problem. One of the first lay pastors, Hermann Garlichs, later returned to Germany for ordination after gathering the first Missouri Evangelical congregations at Femme Osage and St. Charles in 1833. Basel and Barmen missionary societies responded quickly to the need for missionaries to serve the congregations as ministers. They were unconcerned about differing confessional affiliations. Cooperation with the Congregational Home Missionary Society and the American Board of Commissioners for Foreign Missions was initiated in 1836 after Basel pastors George W. Wall and Joseph A. Rieger had spent several months among Congregationalists in Hartford, Connecticut. Traveling to New York, Philadelphia, and points west, their plea for aid yielded funds for Evangelical missions. The pietistic Wall served the incompatible rationalistic Holy Ghost Church, the first German

Church in St. Louis. Abolitionist sympathizer Rieger lived with abolition martyr Elijah Lovejoy in Alton, Illinois and, in 1837, became the first secretary of the Illinois Anti-Slavery Society, while teaching school and serving as an itinerant preacher.

In 1840 the fellowship of pastors and people was organized. In 1849, the first church, St. Paul's in St. Louis, joined the pastoral conference, the Kirchenverein. In 1847, the Kirchenverein produced its own *Evangelical Catechism*, abbreviated in 1862 by Andreas Irion. In 1848, a common confession to the Holy Scriptures as the basis of faith and life, and harmony with the *Augsburg Confession*, Luther's *Small Catechism* and the *Heidelberg Confession* were acknowledged. The intent was not to coerce Christian conscience at points of disagreement, but to provide symbols for the word of God, behind which was the reality of God's redeeming love through Jesus Christ. By 1857, an Agenda (Worship Order) was adopted and in 1862, an Evangelical *Hymnal*.

Among the German immigrants were free-thinking rationalists, who placed their hope in science, education, and culture. Many of them Deists, they clung to their emancipation from the church and, feeling enlightened, instead joined lodges, clubs, and singing societies. Many were disdainful of pastors and churches, contributing needlessly to hardship on the frontier. They were unimpressed by the occasional revivalist who visited their frontier communities. However, when their own children showed signs of illiteracy and irreligion, many were sufficiently disturbed to extend hospitality to a well-trained pastor of true faith, who often had to serve several communities at once.

Parochial schools were for a time more prevalent than Sunday schools, until concern for children's segregation from the community would cause many to close. During the Civil War years, to provide curriculum materials for the parochial schools and Sunday schools, the General Conference authorized the publication of readers, textbooks, a *Christian Children's Paper* and many books, among them, *Biblische Geschichten* (Bible Stories) and a *Sunday School Hymnal* full of chorales, folk melodies and spiritual lieder.

Social and political instability of the 19th-century American frontier aborted several starts to colleges and seminaries needed to train ministers and teachers for the Synods of the West. A college at Washington, Missouri, begun by the Society (Kirchenverein) in 1854, opened in 1858 and died during the Civil War (along with 26 others in the United States), when parents refused to allow their sons to go to the "guerilla-infested" region along the Missouri. Eden Theological Seminary (1850) and Elmhurst College (1871) have endured with distinction.

To assure authenticity and high standards of ministry on the frontier, pastors not yet ordained who sought admission to membership in the Kirchenverein were examined as to their character and their affirmation of the writings of "our Evangelical mother Church in Germany." By 1850, total dependence upon men of German theological training had been relieved by the establishment of a seminary in Marthasville, Missouri, later to become Eden Theological Seminary, a school of distinctive Lutheran and Reformed union-oriented piety. The seminary received financial support from other denominations, from Germany and from friendly benefactors. The new journal, *Der Friedensbote* (Messenger of Peace) helped to unify the church.

Naturally harsh frontier conditions, remnants of Lutheran-Reformed controversies, the arrogance (often cruelty) of the rationalists, and geographical isolation made communications, association, and mutual support urgent. Such difficulties also contributed to the establishment of free, unassociated churches and to the defection of some pastors to join established American denominations. Pietistic Evangelicals, facing some of the same conditions that New England settlers experienced and sharing with the Puritans an ascetic tendency, felt drawn to the Congregationalists and Presbyterians. Congregational leaders such as Horace Bushnell were instrumental in aiding establishment of German Evangelical churches in the West and providing them with ministers from Basel and Barmen. Presbyterians sent teachers and preachers as well.

The primary thrust of Evangelical mission was to establish churches in countryside and city and to serve the needs of the German population in areas west of Ohio. The Board of Home Missions, created in 1870, was called on to assist German-Russian immigrants to Colorado, descendants of Germans who had been asked by the Empress Catherine (the Great) to settle the lower Volga area. They had been promised that their language and culture would be respected and preserved. Abridgement of agreed-upon rights under Nicholas II sent the German-Russian settlers in search of freedom. They came in such numbers that the Board of Home Missions, in 1914, established an academy at Fort Collins to train German-Russian ministers and lay workers. It was closed when World War I cut off the flow of immigrants.

Evangelical churches were grateful recipients of mission society aid. Between 1840 and 1860 they responded with funds, gifts out of proportion to the church population, for the societies at Barmen and Basel that had provided pastors. At home, Evangelical Society missions would focus on needs arising among the German settlements on the frontier. Led by Louis Nollau, an Evangelical hospital was established in St. Louis, and in 1858 200 patients were rejected for lack of space. With community support, the Good Samaritan Hospital opened in 1861. Nollau also reached out to the plight of orphaned and victimized children by taking many into his own home until a proper shelter was provided for their growing number. Parochial school children would contribute pennies to their support through "orphan societies." Nollau and others went on to enlarge the mission to the young, the sick, and the aged.

A General Conference was held at Indianapolis in 1866, at which the name Evangelical Synod of the West replaced the term Kirchenverein. A disciplined and committed natural church leader, Adolph Baltzer, was elected its first president. Two years later, instead of a meeting of the full membership, as in the Old Kirchenverein, a system of delegates, elected by district, was instituted.

As stated by Baltzer, faithfulness, obedience, discipline, and the affirmation, "Christ alone! Faith alone! The Bible alone!" would be the guiding principles and articles of faith of the Evangelical Synod. Baltzer would recognize the ephemeral nature of organizations and institutions, even denominations, but emphasized the enduring and fruitful nature of "work done in the name of the Lord and in his spirit." Baltzer traveled thousands of miles by railroad, steamboat, horse and foot, to visit all the churches and would report, after two years, a 20 percent increase in churches and pastors, an incredible transformation in the land from frontier conditions to prosperous farms abundant with fruit and grain, and an increasing need to attend to the education of children. In 1884, the Evangelical Synod began its foreign missions in India.

Between 1857 and 1872, four unions took place between the Missouri Evangelicals and other church associations. In 1872, the major Synod of the West, the Synod of the East (western New York and Ohio), and the Synod of the Northwest (Illinois, Michigan and Indiana) united. By 1877 the denomination included 324 pastors and became the German Evangelical Synod of North America. By 1934, when the Synod merged with the Reformed Church in the United States, Evangelicals totaled 281,598, pastored by 1,227 clergy.

Two theologians of the 20th century of great influence and acclaim throughout Protestant America were nurtured in the Evangelical Church. Helmut Richard Niebuhr, called a "theologian's theologian," wrote and taught Christian ethics at Yale Divinity School. Educated at Elmhurst College and Eden Seminary as well as Yale Divinity School, his older brother Reinhold Niebuhr became the most influential American theologian since Jonathan Edwards. Pastor of a Detroit church during the difficult anti-German years of World War I, he guided the Evangelical War Welfare Commission to support 25,000 young people from Evangelical churches serving in the American armed forces. While a Union Theological Seminary professor, he wrote books of ethics and theology, among them *Moral Man and Immoral Society* and *The Nature and Destiny of Man*. He became the American exponent of neoorthodoxy, a theology that attempted amidst the declining morality of the 20th century, to reapply biblical teachings and truths to areas of contemporary social and political concern. The Niebuhrs helped to determine the theological orientation of thousands of religious and secular leaders and thereby to help crumble the sectarian walls of division of the Christian world.

By 1929, deep in negotiations on union with the Reformed Church, the German Evangelical Synod dropped from its name, if not its consciousness, the national designation and beame the Evangelical Synod of North America.

An Ecumenical Age

God has moved throughout the 20th century to impel a world-wide movement toward Christian unity, of which the United Church of Christ is but a part. Understood deeply as obedience, the movement is seen more expediently as an antidote to the rising forces of paganism. The ecumenical movement calls the churches to restore their oneness in Christ by union. A divided church is unlikely to convince the world.

Two world wars and religious sectarianism had made clear a need for the church to take seriously its responsibility as agents of God's healing, and in repentance, to acknowledge in its divisions a mutual need for Christ's redemption. The World Council of Churches, Protestant and Orthodox, met at Amsterdam in 1948 under the theme "Man's Disorder and God's Design." In 1961, it merged with the International Missionary Council. The Second Vatican Council at Rome, called by Pope John XXIII, met between 1962 and 1965, with a primary purpose of "peace and unity." Ending with a reemphasis on ecumenicity, the Pope participated in a joint religious service with non-Catholic Christian observers, and resolved to "remove from memory" the events of A.D. 1054 that first split the Christian church "in two great halves," Catholic and Orthodox.

The United Church movement overseas had an early beginning in the South Indian United Church (1908), later to be the Church of South India and the Church of North India. The Church of Christ in China (1927) followed and, much later, in Japan the Kyodan (1941), The United Church of Christ of the Philippines (1948) and the National Christian Council of Indonesia (1950). Common historic missionary roots were celebrated during a 1976 ecumenical visit to four of the United Churches by a delegation from the United Church of Christ, U.S.A., led by its distinguished ecumenist president, Robert V. Moss, recognized as a world church leader.

Between 1900 and 1950, Congregational churches of ten nations united with other denominations, many losing the name "Congregational." Others followed as the United Church movement proliferated.

In the United States, the Congregational Churches had, since 1890, been making overtures of unity toward other church bodies. German "union" (Lutheran-Reformed) churches in western Pennsylvania and in Iowa, recognized and received as German Congregational Churches in 1927, were absorbed and integrated.

Congregational associations during and following World War I received into fellowship Armenian Evangelicals, a refugee remnant of the 19th-century reform movement in the Armenian Apostolic Church in Turkey. During a period of Turkish genocidal persecution of Armenians, thousands escaped to America, many Evangelicals. In the 1980s there were 16 Armenian Evangelical churches holding membership in the United Church of Christ. Locally, the association relationship among churches made it easy to extend congregational fellowship across denominational lines.

Although it frequently stated convictions of unity, the Christian Church (perhaps because of its long travail over its own North-South division and its disinterest in organizational structure) had remained separatist. Correspondence with the Congregationalists led to a meeting in 1926, when a decision to pursue union was taken. On June 27, 1931, at Seattle, Washington, the Christian Church, with a membership of 100,000, including 30,000 members of the 65 churches in its Afro-American Convention, joined with the Congregational Churches of nearly a million members. They saw their temporal organization of Christian believers as one manifestation of the church universal, a denomination that they intended would remain adaptable, so as to enable a faithful response to the biblical Word of God in any time, in any place, among any people.

Such an understanding of the church had also matured in the Evangelical and the Reformed churches from seeds planted centuries before in Switzerland and Germany and replanted in America by the Mercersburg movement. With resolve strengthened by the great ecumenical assemblies, in 1918 the Reformed Church in the United States, led by George W. Richards, produced a *Plan of Federal Union* in hope of uniting churches of the Reformed heritage. Similarly inspired, Samuel Press, supported by the local churches represented at the 1925 General Conference, led the Evangelical Synod of North America to undertake negotiations looking toward organic union. While other communions of shared tradition had become involved, by 1930, only the Reformed Church and the Evangelical Synod pursued their long-hoped-for union.

After six years of negotiation, a *Plan of Union* evolved, approved in 1932 by the General Synod of the Reformed Church, ratified by the Evangelical Synod at its General Convention of 1933. Significant and unprecedented was the decision to unite and then to work out a constitution and other structures for im¬plementation, surely an act of Christian obedience and faith in the power of the Holy Spirit to sustain trust in one another. On June 26, 1934, the Evangelical and Reformed Church was born at Cleveland, Ohio.

THE EVANGELICAL AND REFORMED CHURCH

A blend of autonomy and authority, the Evangelical and Reformed Church retained a Calvinist doctrine of the church as "the reality of a kingdom of grace," and the importance of order and discipline in its witness to the reign of God in the world. The *Heidelberg Catechism* still at its heart, the new church would embody a synthesis of Calvin's inward sense of God's "calling" and Luther's experiential approach to faith. George W. Richards, ecumenist first president, had expressed the insights of all Reformation streams by saying, "Without the Christlike spirit, no constitution will ever be effective; with the spirit, one will need only a minimum of law for the administration of the affairs of the fellowship of men and women." In such a spirit the union proceeded without a constitution until one was adopted in 1938, implemented in 1940.

The second president, Louis W. Goebel, a trusted Christian statesman and exponent of the church's freedom in Christ, guided the organization and ecumenical relationships of the 655,000-member Evangelical and Reformed Church for 15 years. Its membership was mainly in New York, New Jersey, Pennsylvania, Maryland, North Carolina, Ohio, Michigan, Indiana, Illinois, Iowa, Wisconsin, Minnesota, Texas, Kentucky, Nebraska, Kansas, and Missouri. James E. Wagner, true to the Reformed tradition, yet responsive to the rapid changes of an era, as third president, led the church into a further fulfillment of its unitive intention.

Meanwhile, the practical act of consolidating Reformed and Evangelical programs, boards, organizations, and publications and coordinating the multiple institutions went forward. The church addressed world-wide suffering during World War II with the War Emergency Relief Commission. *The Hymnal* (1941) and *Book of Worship* (1942) were published. Reformed missions in Japan, China, and Iraq were united under the Evangelical and Reformed Church Board of International Missions. New missions were undertaken through cooperative efforts in Ecuador, Ghana, and western Africa. *The Messenger* became the church publication. Christian education resources soon followed. Organizations united. The Woman's Missionary Society united with the Evangelical Women's Union to become the Women's Guild.

A 1937 study group of St. Louis Evangelical and Reformed and Congregational Christian clergy, led by Samuel J. Press, president of Eden, and Truman Douglass, pastor of Pilgrim Congregational Church, had revealed among the participants a sense of "family." Dr. Press acted on the discovery with a June 1938 telegram to the General Council of the Congregational Christian Churches, "What about a rapprochement between our communions looking forward to union?" The affirmative response of Douglas Horton, minister and executive secretary of the General Council, was followed by four years of private conversations before a public proposal in 1942 would be endorsed by the General Synod of the Evangelical and Reformed Church and the General Council of the Congregational Christian Churches. After ten drafts of a *Basis of Union* were prepared between 1943 and 1949, a special General Synod was called in 1949 to approve the *Interpretations of the Basis*. Approval (249–41) was followed by successful ratification by the 34 synods, by vote of 33–1. A uniting General Synod for the United Church, first set for June 26, 1950, was postponed for seven more years. Under Congregational Christian Church autonomy, some local churches brought a legal injunction, challenging the right of the General Council to participate in a union of the whole church with another. President Richards made clear the Evangelical and Reformed Church's commitment to total unity and wholeness.

The Congregational Christian Churches

The union by the Congregational and Christian churches seemed the most natural in the world, yet most of their life together from 1931–57 concerned the General Council with matters surrounding church union, first its own and then with the Evangelical and Reformed Church.

Yet the work of the church continued. In 1934, the General Council at Oberlin, "stirred by the deep need of humanity for justice, security, and spiritual freedom and growth, aware of the urgent demand within our churches for action to match our gospel, and clearly persuaded that the gospel of Jesus can be the solvent of social as of all other problems," voted to create the Council for Social Action. The Council reflected the focus of continuing Christian concern for service, international relations, citizenship, Japanese-Americans, rural life, and legislative, industrial and cultural relations. The General Council had acted to simplify and economize at a national level the prolific and redundant independent actions by churches and conferences, while maintaining the inherent liberties of the local churches.

State Conferences, led by Superintendents or Conference Ministers, responded to local church requests for pastors, resources in Christian education, youth and adult conferences, and speakers on mission and social concerns. They received funds for mission, helped new church starts, and maintained ecumenical contacts.

Printed literature and communication continued to be essential. In 1930, the Christian Church's *The Herald of Gospel Liberty* merged with *The Congregationalist*, to become Advance. The Pilgrim Press, a division of the Board of Home Missions, continued to publish and distribute books, Christian education curriculum materials, monthly magazines and newspapers, hymnals, worship and devotional material, and resources for education and evangelism.

Nationally, the Women's Fellowship connected the work initiated by women in the churches; the Pilgrim Fellowship provided a network of Christian youth. The Laymen's Fellowship enabled men to carry forward a cooperative ministry.

Congregational Christian and Evangelical and Reformed Church leaders already had begun private conversations about union when German Evangelical Church pastor, Martin Niemoeller was incarcerated in Nazi Germany for preaching the Christian gospel from his prominent Berlin pulpit. He boldly opposed the persecution of Jews. On Christmas Eve, 1938, United States Catholics and Protestants, including Congregational Christian and Evangelical and Reformed leaders, sent a message to the German people. A subtle shift in emphasis had gradually crept among the churches from a desire to evangelize the world to a concern for the needs of human society.

The proposed United Church of Christ tried patience and tested persistence. By far the rockier road to union confronted the Congregational Christian Churches. From before the postponed Uniting General Synod of 1950 until 1957, thousands of hours and dollars were spent on court litigation of suits brought against the General Council by autonomous bodies and individuals of the Congregational Christian Churches. Sustained by a court ruling in 1949, the litigants, defining the General Council as "a representative body" accountable to the churches, maintained that the Council had no power to undertake a union involving the churches. Merger leadership defined the General Council as accountable to itself, "a gathering of Christians under the Lordship of Christ." That interpretation persuaded the court to reverse the ruling on appeal, sustained in 1953.

Truman B. Douglass, who would become general secretary of the United Church Board for Homeland Ministries, pointed to the theological principles of the "Headship of Christ" and the Reformed "priesthood of all believers," that sustained autonomy and fellowship, as basic to the Congregational Christian polity. Therefore it was applicable to the "agencies of fellowship." General Council minister Douglas Horton suggested that the General Council was "a kind of Congregation," and that neither it nor the local church was subordinate to the other.

The most celebrated suit was brought by The Cadman Memorial Congregational Church in Brooklyn on behalf of itselves and other

Congregational Christian churches against Helen Kenyon, moderator of the General Council of the Con¬gregational Christian Churches. Helen Kenyon bore the weight of these litigations with strength, patience and valor. Justice Archie O. Dawson, of the United States District Court for the Southern District of New York opined, "It is unfortunate that ministers and church members, who purport to abide by Christian principles should engage in this long, expensive litigation. ..." Then speaking as a "Christian layman ... in all humility" he urged the parties to the controversy to "give prayerful consideration to 1 Corinthians [6:1, 5–7] when similar controversies arose to trouble the early Christians."[2]

Louis W. Goebel at the 1950 Evangelical and Reformed General Synod had with patience and grace stated, "so long as they continue to extend to us the hand of friendship and fellowship ... we members of a church committed to ... the reunion of Christ's church, are bound to accept that hand."[3]

Ruling against those who would block it, the Court of Appeals issued the assurance that the union "would in no way change the historical and traditional patterns of individual Congregational Christian churches" and that none would be coerced into union. Each member was assured of continuing freedom of faith and manner of worship and no abridgement of congregational usage and practice. The ruling assured the churches that the union would depend on voluntary action taken by independent, autonomous churches.[4]

In the United Church of Christ, the separate denominational ancestral stories are preserved at the Congregational Library in Boston, the Amistad Research Center in New Orleans, Lancaster Theological Seminary, Eden Theological Seminary, and Elon College. The central depository of United Church of Christ historical documents is the UCC Archives located at Church House in Cleveland.

Legally free to proceed with union, uneasiness remained. Congregational Christians needed to clarify the difference between authority and power; while all autonomous units—individuals, churches, and agencies—were endowed with temporal power, none wielded authority over another except through the biblical authority of God in Jesus Christ. Evangelical and Reformed Christians needed reassurance that there would be one body and not just one head, trusting that the Holy Spirit would make of the Covenant, owned by the parts of the body—individuals, churches, and agencies—a whole United Church of Christ. In trust, a joint 1954 meeting of the Congregational Christian Executive Committee and the Evangelical and Reformed General Council (ad interim for the General Synod) affirmed *The Basis of Union with the Interpretations* as a foundation for the merger and sufficient for the drafting of a *Constitution*.

Both communions approached the 1957 Uniting General Synod with fresh leadership. James E. Wagner had succeeded Richards as president of the General Synod in 1953, and on Douglas Horton's resignation in 1955, Fred Hoskins was elected Minister and General Secretary of the General Council. Eight theologians from each uniting communion met to study basic Christian doctrine, theological presuppositions, and doctrinal positions in preparation for the writing of a *Statement of Faith*.

All of the Evangelical and Reformed churches, responding to a responsibility laid upon them by their church tradition, and those Congregational Christian churches that understood the church as a people gathered by Christ moved a step farther toward reunion of the Christian church on June 25, 1957—as, with faith in God and growing trust in one another, they became The United Church of Christ. Some 100,000 members who were unable to accept the union joined The National Association of Congregational Christian Churches or The Conservative Congregational Christian Conference.

The United Church of Christ

On Tuesday, June 25, 1957, at Cleveland, Ohio, the Evangelical and Reformed Church, 23 years old, passionate in its impulse to unity, committed to "liberty of conscience inherent in the Gospel," and the Congregational Christian Churches, 26 years old, a fellowship of biblical people under a mutual covenant for responsible freedom in Christ, joined together as the United Church of Christ. The new church embodied the essence of both parents, a complement of freedom with order, of the English and European Reformations with the American Awakenings, of separatism with 20th-century ecumenism, of presbyterian with congregational polities, of neoorthodox with liberal theologies. Two million members joined hands.

The story of the United Church of Christ is the story of people serving God through the church. Co-President James E. Wagner, graduate of Lancaster Seminary, parish minister, seminary professor, and instructor in Bible, brought intellectual and spiritual stature, wisdom and brotherly warmth to match the generous personality of Co-President Fred Hoskins, gifted Congregational Christian professor and pastor, of liberal theological orientation and consummate organizational ability.

A message was sent to the churches from the Uniting General Synod, signed by its moderators, Louis W. Goebel and George B. Hastings, its co-presidents, and co-secretaries Sheldon E. Mackey and Fred S. Buschmeyer. After acknowledging the separate ancestries of the parties to the union and citing ecumenical "relatives" of both denominations, the message stated, "Differences in ecclesiastical procedure, which in sundry places and times have occasioned tensions and disorders, are appointed their secondary place and are divested of evil effect." The union, the message continued, was possible because the "two companies of Christians hold the same basic belief: that Christ and Christ alone is the head of the Church. ... From him [we] derive the understanding of God, ... participation in the same spirit, the doctrines of faith, the influence toward holiness, the duties of divine worship, the apprehension of the significance of baptism and the Lord's Supper, the observance of church order, the mutual love of Christians and their dedication to the betterment of the world."[5]

A *Joint Resolution*, declaring the basis of union, adopted by both parties at the Uniting General Synod, said in part: "Delegates of the Evangelical and Reformed Church and the General Council of the Congregational Christian Churches, in joint session assembled this day in the city of Cleveland, Ohio, do hereby declare that *The Basis of Union with the Interpretations* has been legally adopted ... that the union ... is now effected under the name of 'The United Church of Christ' ... that the union be formally pronounced ... in the name of the Father, and of the Son, and of the Holy Spirit ... that until the adopting Constitution ... *The Basis of Union* shall regulate the business and affairs of the United Church of Christ..."

The Second General Synod at Oberlin in 1959 received for study by the churches a first draft of a constitution and approved a *Statement of Faith* (see below). Able administration by the co-presidents and intensive committee work by lay and clergypersons produced an orderly procedure for consolidation of boards and other program agencies.

STATEMENT OF FAITH

We believe in God, the Eternal Spirit, Father of our Lord Jesus
Christ and our Father, and to his deeds we testify:
    He calls the worlds into being, creates man in his own image,
        and sets before him the ways of life and death.
    He seeks in holy love to save all people from aimlessness
        and sin.
    He judges men and nations by his righteous will
        declared through prophets and apostles.
    In Jesus Christ, the man of Nazareth, our crucified and
        risen Lord, he has come to us
        and shared our common lot,
        conquering sin and death
        and reconciling the world to himself.
    He bestows upon us his Holy Spirit,
        creating and renewing the church of Jesus Christ,
        binding in covenant faithful people of all ages,
        tongues, and races.
    He calls us into his church
        to accept the cost and joy of discipleship,
        to be his servants in the service of men,
        to proclaim the gospel to all the world
        and resist the powers of evil,
        to share in Christ's baptism and eat at his table,
        to join him in his passion and victory.
    He promises to all who trust him

forgiveness of sins and fullness of grace,
courage in the struggle for justice and peace,
his presence in trial and rejoicing,
and eternal life in his kingdom which has no end.
Blessing and honor, glory and power be unto him. Amen.

The Third General Synod at Philadelphia in 1961 adopted the *Constitution and By-Laws* and elected a devoted, hardworking pastor its first president. Ben Herbster, earnest supporter of educational and ecumenical Christian endeavors, always faithful to the needs and requests of local churches and pastors, would guide the "freedom and order" of the new church for eight years. Calling for unity, he would, in his own words, remain "experimental ... seeking new modes that speak to this day in inescapable terms."

The youthful years of the United Church of Christ called the church to ministry in a society barely recovered from a war in Korea, soon thrust with its burden of sorrow and guilt into another in Vietnam. Burgeoning and expensive technologies in a shrinking world seemed to offer the bright prospect of ever more familiar human relationships, with fleeting promises of time to enjoy them, yet generating ominous clouds of increasing crime, violence and fear of nuclear annihilation. The first years of the church's life began during a period of unprecedented national economic prosperity and hope, when, during the preceding decades, new church buildings had abounded to accommodate worshipers disinclined to consider denomination important.

The initial constitution provided for the General Synod to recognize the United Church Board for Homeland Ministries and the United Church Board for World Ministries as mission instrumentalities. Also recognized to do the work of the church were the Pension Boards and the United Church Foundation. Other program instrumentalities for the whole work of the church established, as needed, directly by the General Synod were: Stewardship Council, Office of Communication, Office for Church in Society, and Office for Church Life and Leadership.

The General Synod also created special bodies such as the Commission for Racial Justice, Commission on Development, Coordinating Center for Women in Church and Society, Historical Council, Council for Ecumenism, and Council for Higher Education. It provided for a Council of Conference Ministers comprised of the executives of the 39 conferences. It acknowledged a Council of Instrumentality Executives for the purpose of assisting the president and Executive Council in planning implementation of General Synod and Executive Council (acting ad interim for General Synod) decisions.

The priorities, pronouncements, and program recommendations of the General Synods throughout the 1960s and 1970s reflected a biblical sensitivity to God's care for a world that once led Jesus of Nazareth to weep over the city of Jerusalem. Peace, ecumenism, and human rights walked hand in hand in the United Church of Christ during the 1960s, continuing into the 1970s, the last with a louder and louder voice. At the grassroots, many people worked for black and other minority justice rights, for the elevation of women to equal regard and opportunity with men in society, for just treatment and consideration of all persons of whatever sexual orientation, for a more humane criminal justice system, and for affirming the rights of persons with disabilities to lead a full life in a church and society assessable to all. Local churches were encouraged to support local councils of churches and the work of the National Council of Churches of Christ in the United States, that had in 1950 united many efforts of Protestant and Orthodox churches.

On the national level, a Consultation on Church Union (COCU) was initiated in 1960 through an invitation to four denominations, including the United Church of Christ, to "form a plan of church union both catholic and reformed." Other churches sympathetic to the proposal were invited to join the endeavor and the descriptive phrase was altered to read "catholic, evangelical and reformed."

In 1966, COCU produced *Principles of Church Union*. And in 1970, COCU offered the nine member communions an ambitious Plan of Union for institutional merger that was subsequently rejected. Between 1976–1984, a third text was developed and critiques by the member churches and four *"Alerts"* were added to identify contemporary church-dividing issues, including racism, sexism, institutionalism and exclusivism in congregations. The revised document was published in 1984 as *The COCU Consensus: In Quest of a Church of Christ Uniting.* The member churches labored to honor the Lund Faith and Order Conference's counsel that churches "would not do anything alone that could be done as well or better with other churches."

International confessional bodies also sought closer relations that led to the union in 1970 of the Alliance of Reformed Churches throughout the World holding the Presbyterian System (1875) and the International Congregational Council (1891) as the World Alliance of Reformed Churches (WARC). The United Church of Christ, with both congregational and reformed lineage, is an active member of WARC.

In 1972 *United Church Herald* joined *Presbyterian Life* to become *A.D.* The same inclusive spirit became prominent within the denomination as well. In an attempt to bring young people more fully into the life of the church, the two former national youth structures (Pilgrim Fellowship and Youth Fellowship) were abandoned. In 1969, the Seventh General Synod voted that a minimum of 20 percent of all future Synod delegates and members of national boards must be under 30 years of age. This action has led many conferences, associations, and churches to include youth in decision-making bodies.

Increasing numbers of young people attend General Synods as visitors as well as delegates. Delegates under 30 have strongly influenced decisions. Articulate, committed young people have inspired and given new life to the General Synods since 1969. A National Youth Event, usually held every four years but not in the same year as General Synod, rallies 2000 or more youth leaders of the United Church of Christ on a college campus for worship, debate, Bible study, service projects and fellowship. No longer are young people seen as "the church of tomorrow;" they are an integral part of the church today throughout the denomination.

During a period of student unrest, strong protest of America's involvement in the Vietnam War, continuing pressure for minority rights, the initial upheavals of the women's movement, and following national outrage and grief over assassinations of public leaders, North Carolinian Robert V. Moss, New Testament scholar and president of Lancaster

Theological Seminary, was elected president of the United Church of Christ by the General Synod in 1969. Greatly loved, a gentle man with firm biblical conviction, he spoke with a loud anti-war voice and guided faithfully the church's peace and justice efforts. With a General Synod mandate, he called for withdrawal from Vietnam and for support of United States policies that would lessen rivalries in the Middle East. An advocate of ecumenism, he served with distinction on the Central Committee of the World Council of Churches and supported its stands against apartheid in South Africa and for world peace.

General Synod VIII, concerned also with the faith crisis, racial justice, peace and United States power, and the local church, established a Task Force on Women in Church and Society, which pressed successfully for a General Synod mandate that 50 percent of delegates to national meetings and members on national boards and councils be women, and later for use of inclusive language in the church.

The Council for American Indian Ministries (CAIM), Pacific and Asian American Ministries (PAAM), and the Council for Hispanic Ministries look after special needs and interests of their minority groups and offer their unique gifts of ministry to the rest of the church.

From the General Synod in 1973, a delegation of 95 flew from St. Louis to the Coachella Valley in California to stand with the United Farm Workers in their struggle against farm owners and a rival union. The General Synod responded to the financial crisis of six black American Missionary Association-founded colleges in the South, by raising $17 million through the bicentennial 17/76 Achievement Fund campaign between 1974 and 1976. The fund also aided overseas educational institutions. The same General Synod voted bail money for the "Wilmington 10," a group of eight young black men and one white woman who, involved in a North Carolina racial conflict, were imprisoned with a United Church of Christ worker, who was sent by the Commission for Racial Justice to help.

In the autumn of 1976, the church mourned the death from illness of its 54-year-old second president. Robert V. Moss died on October 25. Feeling keenly their loss, the churches received gladly his legacy of concern for justice, peace, and ecumenism.

Joseph H. Evans, secretary of the United Church of Christ, led the church as its third president for an interim period of 11 months. He repeatedly carried across America and over-seas a message of unity and purpose to the grieving church and with pastoral skill brought comfort to many people.

Disintegration in the culture of traditional Christian mores surrounding sexual relationships and the institutions of marriage and family raised the need for a church study of human sexuality. Differing perspectives on biblical teaching rendered the study controversial. The General Synod in 1975 and 1977 sustained the conviction that sexual and affectional orientation should not be a basis for denial of human rights enjoyed by others.

In 1977, the General Synod chose a vigorous former pastor and Massachusetts Conference minister, Avery D. Post, as president. A New Englander of poetic appreciations and ecumenical faith, grounded in a neoorthodox biblical theology, he was elected by acclamation.

The synod also called the church to responsible monitoring of exploitative broadcasting, public access and opportunity for handicapped persons, and the right to meaningful, remunerative work. World hunger and a threatened environment were commended to United Church Christians for attention and re-mediation, as was the social responsibility of multinational corporations.

A covenant with the Christian Church (Disciples of Christ) to continue cooperative projects and theological and ecclesiological studies postponed a decision on formal union negotiations until 1985.

United Church Christians provided legal and moral support during the seven years that it took to win vindication for the "Wilmington 10." After a 1979 national women's meeting convened 2,000 women at Cincinnati, the Coordinating Center for Women in Church and Society was established and funded by General Synod XIII.

By 1980, there were 485 United Church of Christ congregations of predominantly minority background, numbering 76, 634 persons of Afro, Asian and Pacific Island, Hispanic, and American Indian heritage. Between 1970 and 1979, each group showed net gains in membership. A decline in general United Church of Christ membership was believed to reflect demographic and migratory patterns in the United States.

Movements within the church such as the United Church People for Biblical Witness, the Fellowship of Charismatic Christians in the United Church of Christ, and United Church Christians for Justice Action help people of like perception and intention to find one another within the "beautiful, heady, exasperating mix" of the pluralistic church.

The church responded to these changes. Recognizing the urgency of Christian renewal and mission, General Synod XIII adopted a four-year program to fund New Initiatives in Church Development. Synod delegates expressed their support for women's equality by participating in vigils to encourage ratification of the Equal Rights Amendment. Peace and Family Life, eloquently upheld by youth delegates, became priorities for the biennium.

General Synod XIV, meeting in Pittsburgh, Pennsylvania, saw the election of the Rev. Carol Joyce Brun as the third Secretary of the United Church of Christ, succeeding Dr. Joseph H. Evans. At General Synod XIV the ministry sections of the Constitution and Bylaws were extensively amended, "Youth and Young Adults" was adopted as a priority, a new Council on Racial and Ethnic Ministries was authorized, a mission partnership with the Presbyterian Church of the Republic of Korea was voted, and such mission issues as the concern for persons with AIDS, justice and peace in Central America, and the evil of apartheid in South Africa received the careful attention of the delegates.

Delegates at General Synod XV, meeting in Ames, Iowa, expressed their concern about the farm crisis in the United States, declared the United Church of Christ a Just Peace Church, supported sanctuary for political refugees escaping from South Africa and Central America, and supported full divestment of all financial resources from all corporations doing business with South Africa.

General Synod XV voted an ecumenical partnership with the Christian Church (Disciples of Christ), a relationship with the Pentecostal Church of Chile and reaffirmed the commitment of the denomination to be a "united and uniting church" through an official response to Baptism, Eucharist and Ministry, a faith and order text published by the World Council of Churches.

Succeeding *A.D.* in 1985 was a new tabloid, the *United Church News.*

In 1987 General Synod XVI affirmed God's continuing covenant with the Jewish people. In the voted resolution any suggestion that the birth of the church involved God's abrogation of the divine covenant with the Jews was firmly disavowed. The delegates deplored anti-Semitism and urged closer relations with the Jewish people. At General Synod XVII in 1989, the delegates approved a similar resolution calling for a positive relationship between the United Church of Christ and the Muslim Community.

General Synod XVII also voted to relocate the headquarters of the United Church of Christ from New York City to Cleveland, Ohio, effective January 1990. One of the first responsibilities entrusted to Paul H. Sherry, elected as President at this General Synod, was to shepherd the relocation process with the assistance of the Executive Council and the two recognized instrumentalities (UCBHM and UCBWM). The delegates approved a pronouncement and plan of action on the Christian faith and economic justice, authorized the process for the UCBHM to prepare a new hymnal and adopted the Consensus document of the *Consultation on Church Union.*

In 1991 General Synod XVIII approved a pronouncement and plan of action in support of universal health care in our nation. In response to concerns raised by indigenous Hawaiians and others, a public apology for the role of our national government and church leaders in the overthrow of Queen Lili'uokalani and her lawful government in 1893 was approved. On January 17, 1993 President Sherry delivered the public apology in Honolulu on the occasion of the centennial anniversary of the overthrow of the Queen. The delegates affirmed as well the right of self-determination for the people of Puerto Rico and asked President Sherry to make pastoral visits to Puerto Rican prisoners of conscience incarcerated in our federal prisons. The first visit was made in the winter of 1992–93 at the federal prison for women in Dublin,

California.

At General Synod XIX in 1993 the delegates approved a pronouncement and plan of action inviting the entire denomination to become more intentionally an inclusive multiracial and multicultural church accessible to all. On this occasion, the mutual recognition and reconciliation of the ordained ministries of the United Church of Christ and the Christian Church (Disciples of Christ) were celebrated as an expression of the partnership previously adopted. The delegates debated the role of inclusive language in work then being done on a new hymnal, affirmed that children may be invited to share fully in all worship, including reception of the sacrament of Holy Communion, and expressed support for the United Mine Workers and their right to collective bargaining.

During General Synod XX in 1995, President Sherry and others visited three of the Puerto Rican prisoners of conscience incarcerated at the federal prison for women in Dublin, California. At this Synod, the delegates welcomed and dedicated *The New Century Hymnal* published by The Pilgrim Press. Other actions included the adoption of Churches in Covenant Communion from the Consultation on Church Union, approval of a resolution against violence in media and a resolution on fair and just compensation for church employees. At this Synod, after more than a decade of work, the Committee on Structure was thanked for its leadership and dismissed as its report was turned over to a new committee for possible implementation.

In 1997 General Synod XXI approved the Formula of Agreement, establishing full communion among the United Church of Christ, the Evangelical Lutheran Church in America, the Presbyterian Church (USA) and the Reformed Church in America. This action was the fruit of almost four decades of negotiations and agreements published in *A Common Calling*. The delegates called for the closing of the School of the Americas in protest against its role in legitimizing fear, intimidation and torture in the internal struggles of nations in Central and South America.

At this Synod the delegates received the *Report on Restructure* prepared by the Transition Coordinating Committee and the Constitution and Bylaws Revision Team. The time line for restructuring was approved and revisions to the Constitution related to the new structure were voted and sent to the Conferences and the recognized instrumentalities that subsequently ratified them.

General Synod XXII in 1999 approved amendments to the Bylaws related to the new structure. It elected the initial five leaders who constitute the Collegium of Officers of the four covenanted ministries, provided a means for them to begin their preliminary and consultative work on January 1, 2000 and set their terms to begin on July 1, 2000. John H. Thomas was elected General Minister and President. Other voted actions included resolutions on the abolition of the death penalty, recommitment to interfaith collaboration, and opening the question of multiple tracks of preparation for licensed and ordained ministry. On August 11, 1999 the Puerto Rican prisoners of conscience on whose behalf the General Synod had advocated release were pardoned by the Clinton white house.

In March 2000 the replica of the Amistad ship was launched in Mystic, Connecticut, with the United Church of Christ as one of four partners who made the project possible. In May the Amistad Chapel was dedicated at Church House and in June a festive public celebration inaugurating the new structure was held in Cleveland. In the months that followed, General Ministries, Justice and Witness Ministries, Local Church Ministries and Wider Church Ministries, all covenanted ministries of the United Church of Christ, organized themselves and continued without interruption the programs and services of the previous instrumentalities.

In 2001 General Synod XXIII met jointly with the Assembly of the Christian Church (Disciples of Christ). On this occasion, both denominations voted to become members of Churches Uniting in Christ, along with seven other denominations, as recommended by the Consultation on Church Union after four decades of deliberation. General Synod also celebrated an emerging ecumenical relationship with the Alliance of Baptists, appealed for appropriate international action to address the HIV/Aids pandemic in Africa, affirmed the public education rights of children in our nation as we enter the twenty-first century and endorsed embryonic stem cell research.

At General Synod XXIV in 2003 the delegates celebrated the decision of the United States military to cease bombing exercises on the island of Vieques, Puerto Rico, and to return the land to civilian use. They reaffirmed our historic relationship of intercommunion (*kirchengemeinschaft*) with the Evangelical Church of the Union as it joined the larger Union of Evangelical Churches in Germany, and extended that relationship to the new body. Other actions included approval of a new partnership in mission and ministry with the Alliance of Baptists, full communion with the Church of South India and a call for the end of violence not only against gays and lesbians but transgender persons as well.

General Synod XXV in 2005 celebrated the "God is still speaking" initiative, a public media endeavor through commercial television, to share the inclusive church identity of the United Church of Christ. This ongoing ministry centered in the extravagant welcome that God expects of the church has increased exponentially the inquiries addressed to the website (www.ucc.org) and the number of persons visiting our local churches. The delegates welcomed almost one hundred local churches started, renewed or received from other traditions in the biennium since the previous General Synod. Two thirds of the congregations are from racial, ethnic, multiracial and multicultural backgrounds and one third are Open and Affirming.

Voted actions included approval of multiple tracks of preparation for ordained ministry, criticism of the state of Israel for the wall constructed in the occupied West Bank, endorsement of fair trade practices through the purchasing power of our denomination and support for equal marriage rights and responsibilities for same-gender couples. It laid groundwork for observing the fiftieth anniversary of the United Church of Christ in 2007.

The United Church of Christ, through the office of general ministries and its ecumenical desk, in cooperation with the other covenanted ministries, conferences, associations, local churches and individual members participates actively in the ecumenical movement. Communication and visitation are sustained with Christian leaders, lay and ordained, throughout the world, including those in the Soviet bloc, the war-torn Middle East, developing countries, and especially in partnership with united and uniting churches of Christ. The church remains a member of the National Council of Churches, the World Council of Churches and the World Alliance of Reformed Churches.

The United Church of Christ continues to be a united and uniting church. God alone is its author; Christ alone is its head. A biblical church, it continues to witness by the power of the Holy Spirit, remembering that "truths hitherto guarded in separateness become imperiled by their separateness because they are in essence 'catholic' truths, not 'sectarian.'"

The Relationships and Functions

LOCAL CHURCHES

The basic unit of the United Church of Christ, a local church is composed of persons who are organized for Christian worship and for the ongoing work of Christian witness. All persons who are members of a local church of the United Church of Christ are thereby members of the United Church of Christ.

ASSOCIATIONS

Situated within a conference, an association consists of all local churches in a geographical area, all ordained ministers holding standing therein, all commissioned ministers of that association, and those licensed ministers granted vote. Associations determine the standing of local churches in the United Church of Christ and grant, transfer, and terminate ordained ministerial standing in the United Church of Christ.

CONFERENCES

A conference consists of all local churches in a geographical area and all ordained ministers, commissioned ministers, or licensed ministers holding standing or vote in its associations (or in the conference itself when acting as an association). These, as well as delegates selected by local churches of the conference, may vote when the conference meets. The standing and geographical boundaries of a conference as a body of the United Church of Christ are determined by the General Synod.

GENERAL SYNOD

THE GENERAL SYNOD, the representative body of the United Church of Christ, consists of delegates chosen by the conferences; thirty members of each board of directors of the four covenanted ministries; and ex officio delegates. It carries on the work of the United Church of Christ; provides for the financial support of this work; calls and elects officers of the denomination; nominates and elects members of boards of directors of covenanted ministries; nominates and elects most Executive Council members; establishes and maintains the United Church of Christ's national headquarters; receives and disburses funds contributed for the support of the United Church of Christ and its covenanted ministries; and determines ecumenical and interchurch relationships.

THE EXECUTIVE COUNCIL, which acts for the General Synod ad interim, consists of members named by the Synod plus representatives of covenanted ministries and other United Church of Christ bodies and groups. It coordinates and evaluates the work of the United Church of Christ; is responsible for policies related to the church's mission in its national setting, including the health of the covenanted ministries in relationship with one another and their accountability to the Synod; supports the church's spiritual and financial health; performs corporate functions of the Office of General Ministries; facilitates the Synod's business; and is a focal point for planning and budgeting.

# of The United Church Of Christ

COVENANTED MINISTRIES

There are four covenanted ministries of the United Church of Christ, each carrying out its work in covenantal relationship with the General Synod and Executive Council and in interactive partnership with local churches, associations, conferences, and national bodies of the church. Each nominates for election by General Synod its executive minister who participates in the Collegium of Officers. Each has its own budget, charter and bylaws. Each participates in the Mission Planning Council.

JUSTICE AND WITNESS MINISTRIES enables and encourages all settings of the church to engage in God's mission globally by direct action for the integrity of creation, justice, and peace. It encourages and assists the church in speaking prophetically on matters of justice, power, and public policy and confronting racism, ageism, classism, and other expressions of injustice and alienation. It supports the ministry of service on behalf of the poor, forgotten, oppressed, and those marginalized by stigma and discrimination based on sexual orientation or disability. It may witness on behalf of Synod policies.

LOCAL CHURCH MINISTRIES encourages and supports local churches in the fulfillment of God's mission. It encourages them to shape their life and mission in partnership with one another and with other expressions of the church. It promotes the vocation of all members and the leadership of laity and clergy and facilitates a system of placement. It nurtures stewards and coordinates and promotes church wide mission funding. It strives for the vitality of local churches as inclusive, accessible communities of mission, evangelism, church development, education, unity, worship, nurture, and justice. It also includes The Pilgrim Press and United Church Press and United Church of Christ Resources, the distribution center.

THE OFFICE OF GENERAL MINISTRIES cares for the spiritual life, unity, and well-being of the church; nurtures its covenantal life and its ecumenical and interfaith relationships; and facilitates the visioning, planning, coordination, and implementation of the total mission of the church.

WIDER CHURCH MINISTRIES encourages and supports the United Church of Christ as part of the global church and encourages support of United Church of Christ ministries around the world and the nation. It strengthens relationships with partner churches. It oversees participation in the Common Global Ministries Board, a joint venture with the Christian Church (Disciples of Christ), and, through it, the sending and receiving of missionaries. It supports institutional ministries in health care, education, disaster relief, and social services; coordinates volunteer ministries; and pro-motes interfaith dialogue, global education, and advocacy.

ASSOCIATED AND AFFILIATED MINISTRIES

THE PENSION BOARDS—United Church of Christ, an affiliated ministry of the United Church of Christ, provides employee benefit and ministerial welfare programs.

UNITED CHURCH FOUNDATION, INC., an associated ministry of the Executive Council, offers a broad range of United Church of Christ investment opportunities to strengthen mission.

Covenanted Ministries and Other Bodies

The sections that follow briefly describe the mandates and functions of the United Church of Christ's General Synod, Executive Council, covenanted ministries, and other national bodies as outlined on pages 70–71.

GENERAL SYNOD

The General Synod, a representative body, approves the budget of the United Church of Christ, and nominates and elects the officers of the church, the board members of the covenanted ministries, and the Executive Council. It maintains the treasury for the United Church of Christ, determines ecumenical relationships, and adopts and amends the Constitution and Bylaws of the United Church of Christ.

The General Synod meets every two years in a place deter-mined by the Executive Council. The Synod has between 795 and 845 voting delegates. They come from each conference (675 to 725 delegates) and the four covenanted ministries (30 of each for a total of 120 delegates). Each conference uses its own election procedures to choose delegates. The delegates from the covenanted ministries are chosen from the membership of the boards of directors of General Ministries, Justice and Witness Ministries, Local Church Ministries, and Wider Church Ministries.

As the General Synod gathers, the whole United Church of Christ meets in its diversity to celebrate, to worship, and to conduct the business of the church.

EXECUTIVE COUNCIL

The Executive Council acts for the General Synod ad interim. In cooperation with the officers of the church, it provides coordination and evaluation of the work of the church and is a focal point for decisionmaking, planning, evaluation, and budgeting in the national setting. It is responsible for policies relating to the mission of the United

Church of Christ in its national setting. Among these are policies contributing to the health of the covenanted ministries in relationship with one another and their accountability to General Synod.

The Executive Council supports the spiritual and financial health of the church; receives reports from the Collegium of Officers and provides that body with oversight and support; and performs the legal functions of the Office of General Ministries. The Executive Council schedules and prepares the agenda for all meetings of the General Synod and serves as the Synod's Business Committee and Committee of Reference. It receives and reports upon divergent points of view and maintains an open channel for the consideration of minority or dissenting opinions.

Acting as Budget Committee for the General Synod, the Executive Council prepares and submits to each Synod a biennial United Church of Christ budget for the support of Our Church's Wider Mission. It determines allocations that implement the actions of the General Synod.

The Executive Council has between seventy-six and seventy-eight voting members who are clergy and laypeople elected by the General Synod. They include a member from each of the thirty-nine conferences and three covenanted ministry boards; a youth of high-school age (elected at-large); and one representative from each of the groups listed below under Affiliated and Associated Ministries (see page 77) and Other National Bodies (see page 78). In addition, the Executive Council has the following ex officio members, with voice and vote, who are affirmed by the General Synod:

- The five officers of the United Church of Christ
- The moderator and two assistant moderators of the General Synod
- A member designated by the Christian Church (Disciples of Christ)
- Six conference ministers, chosen by the Council of Conference Ministers
- The executive of United Church Foundation, Inc.
- The executive of The Pension Boards— United Church of Christ

Covenanted Ministries

There are four covenanted ministries of the United Church of Christ. Based at the church's national offices in Cleveland, Ohio, all four of the covenanted ministries work to:

- Proclaim the Good News of Jesus Christ in word and deed to all the world.
- Center the life and work of the United Church of Christ in theological reflection.
- Be faithful and effective instruments for God's mission.
- Take part in the ministry of evangelism within and beyond the church.
- Invite others to help the United Church of Christ become a more intentionally inclusive church that is multiracial, multicultural, and accessible to all.
- Support the founding, development, nurture, and renewal of local churches, in partnership with conferences.
- Minister to and with persons of all generations and all sexual orientations.
- Incorporate women's perspectives and gifts and address women's needs in church and society.
- Develop and nurture leaders for the United Church of Christ.
- Develop resources.

Each of the four also has particular responsibilities.

THE OFFICE OF GENERAL MINISTRIES

The Office of General Ministries cares for the spiritual life, unity, and well-being of the church; nurtures its covenantal life; guides its pilgrimage as a multiracial, multicultural church, accessible to all; provides regular processes that focus on theological reflection throughout the church; and facilitates the envisioning, planning, implementation, and coordination of the United Church of Christ's total mission. It does so through four ministry teams, focusing on:

- Proclamation, identity, and communications
- Covenantal relationships—including racial/ethnic, ecumenical, conference, and other relationships.

- Financial development
- Common services

JUSTICE AND WITNESS MINISTRIES

Justice and Witness Ministries helps the United Church of Christ engage in God's mission by direct action for the integrity of creation, justice, and peace as a global, multiracial, multicultural church, accessible to all. It does so by encouraging collaboration among local churches, associations, conferences, and national bodies of the church. Justice and Witness Ministries acts as a catalyst for God's mission in the world, responding to the world's realities of injustice and oppression, and works for liberation and transformation of systems and persons. It continues the United Church of Christ's historic presence in such places as Washington, D.C., and Franklinton Center, North Carolina, and continues historic support of such institutions as the Amistad Research Center in New Orleans, Louisiana. Justice and Witness Ministries carries out this work through four ministry teams, focusing on:

- Economic justice
- Racial justice
- Human rights, justice for women, and transformation
- Public life and social policy

LOCAL CHURCH MINISTRIES

Local Church Ministries encourages and supports the local churches of the United Church of Christ in fulfillment of God's mission. It supports local churches in their core city, urban, suburban, town, and rural settings and collaborates with local churches, conferences, associations, and related institutions of the United Church of Christ. It supports the pilgrimage of the United Church of Christ as a multiracial, multicultural church, accessible to all, as it is lived out in and through the local church. It does so through five ministry teams, focusing on:

- Worship and education
- Evangelism
- Parish life and leadership
- Stewardship and church finances
- Publications, resource production, and distribution services

WIDER CHURCH MINISTRIES

Wider Church Ministries helps the United Church of Christ participate in the global, multiracial, multicultural church, working toward a church that is accessible to all, and encourages the church to support our ministries around the world and the nation. It does so by encouraging, supporting, and interacting with local churches, associations, conferences and national bodies of the church. Wider Church Ministries also works with the Christian Church (Disciples of Christ) and other ecumenical partners in North America and throughout the world. Wider Church Ministries does this work through five ministry teams, focusing on:

- Wellness empowerment and advocacy
- Mission education and volunteer services
- Partner relations
- Global education and advocacy
- Global ministries and local churches

The last three of these teams particularly work in the context of the United Church of Christ's partnership with the Christian Church (Disciples of Christ) and the Common Global Ministries Board of those two denominations.

Affiliated and Associated Ministries
THE PENSION BOARDS—UNITED CHURCH OF CHRIST

The Pension Boards are an affiliated ministry of the United Church of Christ. They make available a system of employee benefit programs designed to assist ministers and lay workers in achieving financial security during working and retirement years.

The General Synod recognized the responsibility of all congregations and church-related organizations to provide pension benefits for clergy by including this obligation in the call to a minister and has urged all churches to enroll lay employees in the Retirement Fund. The Pension Boards receive a share of Our Church's Wider Mission (OCWM) budget, which is used primarily for the administration of the General Synod's Plan of Supplementation of Small Annuities.

The Pension Boards administer retirement benefits and disability, life, and health insurance. For retirees with special needs, it may also provide, in consultation with conference staffs, emergency help and pension supplementation. These are made possible by the annual Christmas Fund Appeal and the United Church Board for Ministerial Assistance, one of six corporations that compose The Pension Boards.

UNITED CHURCH FOUNDATION, INC.

Established in 1954, the United Church Foundation is an affiliated ministry of the Executive Council. It manages long-term investments for conferences, associations, churches, and other entities related to the United Church of Christ. The fundamental goals of the foundation are to invest assets in a manner that preserves capital, ameliorates the erosive effects of inflation, and provides increases in value in real terms. To implement these goals, the Investment Department staff works under the direction of the Finance Committee which is comprised of highly competent individuals from the financial world who volunteer their knowledge and expertise free of charge.

The governing body of the Foundation is mindful of the corporate social responsibility concerns of the church as it carries out its fiduciary responsibility to the funds under management. Funds are invested on a long-term basis, with careful attention paid to the major social, political, and economic trends that affect investment decisions.

Other National Bodies

Many councils, commissions, coalitions, and special-interest groups—some created by the General Synod, some self-created—have emerged over the years to fulfill specific purposes and needs in the United Church of Christ. The following, in addition to covenanted, affiliated, and associated ministries, are represented on the Executive Council. The Bylaws of the United Church of Christ describe each of these groups as "related in covenant" to the United Church of Christ through a primary relationship with one of the covenanted ministries.

Groups Created by the General Synod

COUNCIL FOR AMERICAN INDIAN MINISTRY. Created by the General Synod in 1987, CAIM provides Christian ministry and witness in American Indian settings and helps the whole United Church of Christ understand and support American Indian churches and communities. It helps American Indian members and congregations embody their cultures and values and be vital parts of the church. CAIM receives one-third of the net income of the Neighbors in Need offering.

COUNCIL FOR ECUMENISM. Composed of twelve persons elected by the Executive Council, the Council for Ecumenism advises the general minister and president. It assists the general minister and president and the Executive Council prepare ecumenical and interfaith policies, determine levels of contribution to ecumenical agencies and activities, and keep the United Church of Christ's commitment to be "united and uniting" before its members and other churches.

COUNCIL FOR HIGHER EDUCATION. Consisting of academies, colleges, and theological schools related to the United Church of Christ, the council advances and interprets higher educational concerns within the church. It cultivates closer relationships between the church and educational institutions; the expression of the connection between faith and knowledge in those institutions; and the promotion of education as an integral part of the church's mission.

COUNCIL FOR RACIAL AND ETHNIC MINISTRIES. Created by the General Synod in 1983, COREM provides a place where racial and ethnic groups can develop their common agenda; collaborate with program and mission bodies of the church so that resources for racial and ethnic ministries will be effective and relevant; discern appropriate ways by which the gifts of racial and ethnic groups may be available to the church; and advocate racial and ethnic concerns within the church.

COUNCIL FOR THEOLOGICAL EDUCATION. This council fosters cooperation among the seven seminaries of the United Church of Christ and mutual accountability between those seminaries and the church. It periodically reviews the criteria for being designated a seminary of the United Church of Christ and explores ways in which theological education contributes to the church's leadership needs. It includes representatives from seminaries, conferences, and covenanted ministries.

COUNCIL FOR YOUTH AND YOUNG ADULT MINISTRIES. "Youth" is defined as being of high school age or younger; "young adults" are ages nineteen through thirty in addition to younger high school graduates. Some of this council's twenty-two to twenty-six members are elected by the General Synod; others are appointed by racial and ethnic groups. The council advocates and creates networks for youth and young adult ministries to ensure that the gifts and talents of young people are represented throughout the church.

COUNCIL OF CONFERENCE MINISTERS. Consisting of the conference ministers of the thirty-nine conferences, this council maintains close relationships with the officers and national bodies of the church. It selects conference ministers to serve on the boards of covenanted ministries and in other representative positions. It also selects its own chairperson, officers, and committees. The general minister and president is an ex officio member of the council and its cabinet.

HISTORICAL COUNCIL. As an advisor to the general minister and president and the Executive Council, the twelve-member Historical Council helps remind the United Church of Christ of its traditions and takes special interest in United Church of Christ-related archives. It recommends amounts of budget moneys to be contributed to two historical societies, the Congregational Christian and the Evangelical and Reformed. These societies elect six council members; the Executive Council appoints the other six.

SELF-CREATED GROUPS

COUNCIL FOR HEALTH AND HUMAN SERVICE MINISTRIES. This council consists of United Church of Christ-related institutions and programs in health and welfare, including hospitals; homes for children, elders, and those with special needs; and other ministries. CHHSM sets standards for and works with conferences in recognizing such institutions; relating to the covenanted ministries; supporting and nurturing its members; and taking part in secular, ecumenical, and interfaith networks.

COUNCIL FOR HISPANIC MINISTRIES. An autonomous body cooperating with all settings of the church, this council promotes its mission within the United Church of Christ and helps to monitor boards and ministries that deal with concerns and issues important to Hispanics, Latinos, and Latinas in the United States, Puerto Rico, Mexico, and other nations of the Caribbean and Central and South America. It honors the con-texts and cultures of its members and encourages dialogue among all constituencies.

MINISTERS FOR RACIAL, SOCIAL, AND ECONOMIC JUSTICE. This group brings together clergy who advocate on behalf of African Americans in church and society, providing a caucus of ministers for fellowship, for sharing of mutual concerns, and for actions regarding the agenda of the black constituency in the United Church of Christ. MRSEJ challenges, monitors, initiates, and supports the cause of African American involvement in the life of the church.

NATIONAL COMMITTEE ON PERSONS WITH DISABILITIES. Consisting of between twenty-five and fifty "active" and "associate" members, this committee strives for full inclusion of persons with disabilities in the life and mission of the church. It encourages local churches to be open, inclusive, affirming, and accessible in their buildings, worship, education, fellowship, and service. It encourages theological and biblical affirmations of the wholeness of all people.

PACIFIC ISLANDER AND ASIAN AMERICAN MINISTRIES. Organized in 1974 and recognized by the 1975 General Synod, PAAM advocates for the presence, participation, and contributions of Pacific Islander and

Asian Americans in the life of the United Church of Christ. It serves and supports its constituent members and churches, works for greater representation in all church settings, nurtures and develops lay and clergy leadership, and addresses justice issues.

UNITED BLACK CHRISTIANS. Representing the more than fifty thousand African American members of the United Church of Christ, UBC affirms that each person has gifts to offer the church and that each is entitled to full rights and privileges as children of God. It provides voice for all African American members of the church, seeking to preserve and witness to the history and legacy of African American people and churches. UBC is an active advocate for liberation and social justice.

UNITED CHURCH COALITION FOR LESBIAN, GAY, BISEXUAL, AND TRANSGENDER CONCERNS. The coalition consists of United Church of Christ members and friends who affirm that God loves and empowers all persons of all sexual orientations. It seeks justice for, and the inclusion and involvement of, lesbian, gay, bisexual, and transgender Christians in the church. It promotes ministries of pastoral care, education, and advocacy and encourages all settings of the church to become "open and affirming."

The Emblem

The emblem of the United Church of Christ is based on the ancient Christian symbol known as the resurrection Cross of Victory or the Cross Triumphant.

Traditionally, this symbol—the cross surmounted by the crown and all of it atop the orb—signifies the kingship of the Risen Christ over all the world. The orb, representing the world, is divided into three parts to signify Jesus' command to his disciples: "You shall be my witnesses in Jerusalem and in all Judea and Samaria and to the end of the earth."

For the United Church of Christ, this emblem, rich in the traditions of the past and alive with hope for the future, is particularly appropriate. For this reason, there appear on the perimeter of the emblem both the name of the church and the text: "That they may all be one."

Notes

1. E.S. Yockey, Historical Sketch of the Origin and Growth of the Woman's Missionary Societies of the Reformed Church (Alliance, OH: The Woman's Journal, 1898), p. 7.

2. Fred Hoskins, Congregationalism Betrayed or Fulfilled (Newton, MA: Andover Newton Theological School, 1962). Southworth Lecture (paper), pp. 7–8.

3. Louis H. Gunnemann, The Shaping of the United Church of Christ: An Essay in the History of American Christianity (New York: The Pilgrim Press, 1977), p. 41.

4. Hoskins, op. cit., p. 41.

5. "Report on the Uniting General Synod," Advance, July 12, 1957, p. 22.

6. Norman Goodall quoted by Hoskins, op. cit., p. 33.

7. The United Church of Christ section, written by Margaret Rowland Post, 1986; edited in 2005.

Books from United Church Press

Confessing Our Faith

An Interpretation of the Statement of Faith of the United Church of Christ

ROGER I. SHINN

ISBN 0-8298-0866-3 • paper • 132 pages • $13.00

Confessing Our Faith describes the process by which local churches and international dialogue partners produced the original 1959 Statement of Faith.

A History of the Evangelical and Reformed Church

DAVID DUNN, ET AL

INTRODUCTION BY LOWELL H. ZUCK

ISBN 0-8298-0855-8 • paper • 396 pages • $20.00

A detailed single-volume history, *A History of the Evangelical and Reformed Church* recounts the story of the two churches that joined together in 1934 to become the Evangelical and Reform Church which then became, twenty-three years later, a part of the United Church of Christ.

The Shaping of the United Church of Christ

An Essay in the History of American Christianity

LOUIS H. GUNNEMANN

EXPANDED BY CHARLES SHELBY ROOKS

ISBN 0-8298-1345-4 • paper • 272 pages • $20.00

This reissue of a classic interpretive essay of the history of American Christianity and the development of the United Church of Christ has a new foreword and concluding chapter by Charles Shelby Rooks. This expanded edition brings the story of the UCC up-to-date through the end of the twentieth century.

United and Uniting

The Meaning of an Ecclesial Journey

LOUIS H. GUNNEMANN

ISBN 0-8298-0757-8 • paper • 220 pages • $17.00

Louis Gunnemann suggests that the history of the modern ecumenical movement is the needed perspective for a fresh renewed understanding of the vision of the UCC.

The Living Theological Heritage of the United Church of Christ

Barbara Brown Zikmund, Series Ed.

A seven volume scholarly series of foundational documents, treatises, statements, and commentaries that chronicle the history, faith, and practice of the United Church of Christ and its predecessor entities.

Complete Seven-Volume Set
ISBN 0-8298-1461-2 • cloth • $350.00

Volume 1

Ancient and Medieval Legacies

Reinhard Ulrich, Ed.

ISBN 0-8298-1143-5 • cloth • 600 pages • $50.00

Volume 2

Reformation Roots

John B. Payne, Ed.

ISBN 0-8298-1143-5 • cloth • 696 pages • $50.00

Volume 3

Colonial and National Beginnings

Charles Hambrick-Stowe, Ed.

ISBN 0-8298-1109-5 • cloth • 640 pages • $60.00

Volume 4

Consolidation and Expansion

Elizabeth C. Nordbeck and Lowell H. Zuck, Eds.

ISBN 0-8298-1110-9 • cloth • 576 pages • $60.00

Volume 5

Outreach and Diversity

Margaret Lamberts Bendroth, Lawrence Neal Jones, and Robert A. Schneider, Eds.

ISBN 0-8298-1111-7 • cloth • 550 pages • $60.00

Volume 6

Growing Towards Unity

Elsabeth Slaughter Hilke, Ed.

ISBN 0-8298-1112-5 • cloth • 786 pages • $70.00

Volume 7

United and Uniting

BARBARA BROWN ZIKMUND AND FREDRICK R. TROST, EDS.

ISBN 0-8298-1113-3 • cloth • 829 pages • $70.00

To order these or any other resources from United Church Press,
please call or write to:
United Church Press
700 Prospect Avenue East, Cleveland, Ohio 44115-1100
Phone orders: 1-800-537-3394 • Fax orders: 216-736-2206

Please include shipping charges of $6 for the first book
and 75¢ each additional book.
Or order from our web sites at www.thepilgrimpress.com and www.
unitedchurchpress.com.
Prices subject to change without notice.